FROM
MARYLAND
TO
Cooperstown

Lois P. Nicholson

Jimmie Foxx and Babe Ruth, both Maryland-born, were baseball's greatest sluggers of the 1920s and 1930s.

FROM MARYLAND TO Cooperstown

Seven Maryland Natives in Baseball's Hall of Fame

LOIS P. NICHOLSON

TIDEWATER PUBLISHERS
CENTREVILLE, MARYLAND

Library of Congress Cataloging-in-Publication Data

Nicholson, Lois 1949–
    From Maryland to Cooperstown : seven Maryland natives in
  Baseball's Hall of Fame / Lois P. Nicholson. — 1st ed.
        p.   cm.
    Summary: Chronicles the lives and careers of seven native-born
  Marylanders who are enshrined in the National Baseball Hall of Fame:
  Babe Ruth, Vic Willis, Frank Baker, Judy Johnson, Lefty Grove,
  Jimmie Foxx, and Al Kaline.
    ISBN 0-87033-494-8 (hc.)
    1. Baseball players—Maryland—Biography—Juvenile literature.
  2. National Baseball Hall of Fame and Museum—Juvenile literature.
  [1. Baseball players—Maryland.   2. National Baseball Hall of Fame
  and Museum.]   I. Title.
  GV865.A1N53   1998
  796.357′092′0752—dc21
  [B]   98-27250
                                                                  CIP
                                                                   AC

Photographs reproduced with permission from the following:
National Baseball Hall of Fame Library, Cooperstown, N.Y.: frontispiece and pp. 34, 62, 82;
Babe Ruth Museum, Baltimore, Md.: pp. 5, 8, 24, 45, 68, 70, 77, 110, 115; Transcendental
Graphics: pp. 13, 19, 21, 27, 49, 112, 117; Thomas R. Hunt Jr.: pp. 31, 38; Norman Macht:
pp. 36, 79, 85, 104; Sudlersville Train Station Museum: p. 53; Historical Society of Talbot
County: p. 55; Todd Bolton: p. 66; Gil Dunn: pp. 89, 96; Loretta C. Walls: p. 99.

Sketches of ballplayers on chapter title pages by David Aiken.

Manufactured in the United States of America
First edition

To children of all ages who love the game

Contents

Foreword

Maryland and baseball have walked the path of history together. The Old Orioles of the 1890s changed the strategy of the game. Babe Ruth rescued it with his booming bat in the 1920s and Jack Dunn's famous International League team showed a dominance few teams can match. Today Maryland points to the modern Orioles as a model franchise and glories in the great endurance record of Cal Ripken Jr. Over the years, the state has displayed a special pride in all the stars born there.

Lois P. Nicholson writes about the best of these. Her list of native Marylanders who have been elected to the National Baseball Hall of Fame at Cooperstown contains some of the most colorful and the most talented players who ever wore spikes.

For a start, who could be more talented or colorful than the bigger-than-life Babe Ruth, a native of Maryland who also played with the Orioles? Lois gives us an interesting picture of the other Maryland Hall of Famers who missed playing for the Orioles. This list dates back to Vic Willis, who pitched at the turn of the century. Then there's the early home run king, Frank "Home Run" Baker; the hot-tempered left-handed ace, Lefty Grove; the muscular slugger, Jimmie Foxx; the fine third baseman from the Negro leagues, Judy Johnson; and the great Detroit Tiger outfielder and batting champion, Al Kaline.

Lois's touch brings to life all these Maryland Hall of Famers. I know you'll enjoy reading about their lives and their exploits in this fine presentation.

—Ernie Harwell, Baseball Hall of Fame broadcaster

Preface

The National Baseball Hall of Fame in Cooperstown, New York, is known as the game's Shrine of Immortals. Many major leaguers dream of receiving baseball's highest honor, yet few men realize that dream. A Hall of Fame player must distinguish himself as one of the sport's elite, not merely a great player, but the best of the great.

Seven players born in Maryland have been inducted into the Hall, a little known fact of which Marylanders can be extremely proud. I hope this book will help inform readers about the state's rich baseball legacy and will turn their attention to the not-too-distant future when Maryland can boast that eight native sons are members of Baseball's Hall of Fame.

Cooperstown's most famous member is Babe Ruth. More than sixty years after he last swung a bat, Ruth remains first in the hearts and memories of baseball fans. That is why the Babe deserves to lead off this book. The rest of the lineup is presented in chronological order. Their stories reflect the many changes in the game during the past century, yet one simple truth endures—America loves the game of baseball.

For their invaluable assistance with this book I wish to thank the following: Ernie Harwell; Bette Holshey; Thomas R. Hunt, Jr.; J. Suter Kegg; Judge James S. Getty; John Meyers; Gregory J. Schwalenberg, curator of the Babe Ruth Museum; and Matt Zabitka of the *Wilmington News Journal*.

Baseball is continuity.
Pitch to pitch.
Inning to inning.
Game to game.
Series to series.
Season to season.

—Ernie Harwell, *The Game for All America*

I

They ask me what it was I hit and I tell them I don't know except it looked good.

—Babe Ruth

George Herman "Babe" Ruth

As Babe Ruth stepped up to the plate on October 1, 1932, at Chicago's Wrigley Field, Cubs pitcher Charlie Root stared in at the thirty-four-year-old left-handed Yankees slugger. The score was 4 to 4 in the fifth inning; Ruth had already hit a three-run homer off Root in the first inning of this third game of the World Series.

The 50,000 Chicago fans jeered the Babe. The Cubs lined their dugout steps and lobbed insults at Ruth. But jawing never bothered the Babe. He yelled right back at them all. Ruth took the first fastball for a strike. He wagged his right index finger at his taunters, signaling "That's only one."

Root's next two pitches were balls, but his fourth pitch sailed past Ruth for another strike. Babe waved two fingers at the Cubs, then pointed at Root, yelling, "I'm going to knock the next pitch right down your throat."

Root delivered a curve, low and outside, the sweetest pitch the Babe had ever seen. He drove it into the center field bleachers. As he rounded the bases he thumbed his nose at the silent Cubs. The Yankees won the game 7 to 5, and finished a sweep of the Series the next day.

Only one scene from that Series lives on in baseball lore: Ruth's home run in Game 3. One writer claimed that Ruth had pointed to the center field fence before hitting the ball. Another writer repeated the story. Babe went along with it, not claiming that he'd actually pointed at the bleachers, yet not denying it either. Ruth's epic homer became known as the "called shot." "It's a good story," Ruth later said.

George Herman Ruth Jr., the greatest player in baseball history, was born in Baltimore, Maryland, on February 6, 1895, in his maternal grandparents' twelve-foot-wide row house at 216 Emory Street. His parents, George and Kate, owned a saloon near the city's docks, and lived in dingy, cramped quarters upstairs. Before Kate Ruth's death in 1910 at thirty-seven, she had given birth to seven more infants, but only George and a daughter, Mary Margaret (Mamie), survived infancy.

The red brick warehouse of the Baltimore and Ohio Railroad loomed over the neighborhood. Twenty hours a day, six days a week, the Ruths served food and drink to workers from the railroad and the docks. "It was a rough, tough neighborhood," the Babe later said, "but I liked it."

A tall, stocky boy, George Jr. thrived on his mother's German cooking and rapidly outgrew the apartment. Energetic and restless, he roamed the streets while his parents were preoccupied with work. The elder Ruths seldom knew their son's whereabouts. Public parks and vacant lots were nonexistent in the neighborhood. The narrow, cobblestone streets were the only playgrounds for children who dodged trucks, wagons, and horse manure during their daily games of hopscotch, jump rope, and stick ball.

George did not like school. When truant officers notified the Ruths that their son was playing hooky, George's mother instructed Mamie to accompany her big brother to the school's front door and watch him to be sure he went inside. The young girl dutifully obeyed, but her efforts failed. "He'd go in all right and then slip out a side door," she recalled.

Ruth and his pals wandered the neighborhood, sneaking into saloons to snatch cigarettes or scraps of food, or to down the remaining contents of beer and whiskey glasses before dashing out the door. "I learned to fear and hate the coppers and to throw apples and eggs at the truck drivers," he later remembered. "I was a bum when I was a kid. I honestly don't remember being aware of the difference between right and wrong." Unable to control George, Mrs. Ruth reluctantly took the seven-year-old boy to the wrought-iron gates of St. Mary's Industrial School, where she turned him over to the Xaverian Brothers on June 13, 1902. George Herman Ruth Jr. remained at St. Mary's for most of the next twelve years. Kate and Mamie faithfully visited him by trolley car each Sunday afternoon, "rain or shine, snow or blow," until Kate's death in 1910.

St. Mary's provided a home for eight hundred boys who were orphans, delinquents, or the sons of destitute families. Although the Ruths had little money, they paid the school fifteen dollars a month, a large sum in that era, for George's food, clothing, shelter, education, and religious instruction. The boys began each day at 6:00 A.M. and were in their classrooms by 7:30. To help prepare them for eventual employment, the boys worked at trades each afternoon. George tried his hand at cigar-rolling and carpentry before discovering he liked working in the tailor shop, where he joined collars to shirts. Despite being left-handed, he excelled at this craft, earning six cents a shirt from the Oppenheim Shirt Company.

Brother Herman, who headed the school recreation program, remembered George as "pretty big for his age, on the wiry side. He was full of mischief, nothing timid about him; an aggressive, shouting boy, always wrestling around with the others."

Brother Mathias, a 6-foot, 6-inch, 250-pound priest whom the boys referred to as "the boss," enforced the school's strict disciplinary code. George immediately liked the big man, later calling him "the greatest man I've ever known." Brother Mathias recognized that George was a good-natured kid whose boundless energies could be channeled positively through structured activities such as sports.

From March through October the boys played baseball every day. Brother Mathias taught his students the game, throwing a ball into the air and launching fungoes that seemed to enter orbit. "I think I was born as a hitter the first day I ever saw him hit a baseball," Ruth later claimed.

Brother Mathias also drilled the boys in defensive skills, teaching them fundamental plays until they could turn a double play or hit a cutoff man. Many years later, Ruth credited his mentor, "I could hit the first time I picked up a bat, but Brother Mathias made me a fielder."

By 1912, seventeen-year-old George was catching for the St. Mary's Red Sox, the school's championship team. Wearing a mitt on his left hand, he would catch a ball, then thrust the mitt under his right armpit, grab the ball with his left hand, and drill it like a bullet. One day George was laughing at his own team's pitcher as an opposing team whipped St.

Ruth, upper left, *is shown with his team at St. Mary's Industrial School in 1912. A left-handed catcher, he used a right-hander's mitt. In later years, Ruth often returned to the school, hitting fungoes and home runs for the boys. When a fire destroyed some buildings, he arranged for the school band to tour with the Yankees to raise money to rebuild.*

Mary's. Brother Mathias stunned him by telling him to take the mound. "Me?" Ruth humbly responded. "I don't know how to pitch."

But the sage brother countered, "Oh, you must know a lot about it. You know enough to know that your friend here isn't any good. Go ahead out there and show us how it's done."

Once on the mound, George easily found his groove, surprising Brother Mathias and himself. "As soon as I got out there I felt a strange relationship with the pitcher's mound," he later recalled. "It was as if I'd been born out there. Pitching just felt like the most natural thing in the world. Striking out batters was easy."

It was apparent that every aspect of baseball came easily to George. During a game between St. Mary's and Mt. St. Joe in 1913, a Washington Senators pitcher, Joe Engel, looked on. As he returned to Washington that night, he bumped into the Baltimore Orioles owner, Jack Dunn, at the train station. Engel said he'd seen a game that afternoon. Dunn, on a constant lookout for talented prospects, asked if he'd seen anyone worth mentioning.

"Yeah," replied Engel. "There was some orphan asylum from Baltimore playing and they had a young left-handed kid pitching for them who's got real stuff."

"You don't remember his name, do you?" asked Dunn.

Engel responded, "I think they called him Ruth."

On February 14, 1914, Jack Dunn went to St. Mary's where he signed George Herman Ruth to a $600 contract for one season with the Baltimore Orioles, then a minor league club. Now nineteen, the dark-haired young man stood 6 feet, 2 inches tall and weighed 160 pounds. Two weeks later a blizzard struck Baltimore, but the snow didn't stop George from boarding a train headed for the Orioles spring training camp at Fayetteville, North Carolina.

The cloistered life at St. Mary's had given the rookie a childlike curiosity about the world beyond its gates. He had never ridden on a train. The hotel elevator in Fayetteville seemed like the eighth wonder of the world. He bribed the operator for the privilege of riding from top to bottom, pushing the buttons and stopping at every floor.

Ruth always had longed for a bicycle. After borrowing one in Fayetteville, he almost ran down Jack Dunn, who was walking down the street. As the club owner collected himself he snarled at the rookie, "If you want to go back to the home, kid, just keep riding those bikes."

On March 7 Ruth played his first game as a professional when the Orioles divided into two squads for a "scrub" or practice game. Playing shortstop, the tall rookie took his turn at bat with one man on in the second inning. "The next batter made a hit that will live in the memory of all who saw it," reported Baltimore sportswriter Rodger Pippen. "The clouter was George Ruth, the southpaw from St. Mary's school. The ball carried so far to right field that he walked around the bases."

Ruth also pitched the final two innings, impressing everyone with his skill at working hitters and his poise when pitching out of the stretch. But it was the home run the southpaw later remembered. "I hit it as I hit all the others," he said, "by taking a good gander at the pitch, twisting my body into a backswing, and then hitting it as hard as I could swing."

"He has all the earmarks of a great ballplayer," Jack Dunn told reporters. "He hits like a fiend and he seems to be at home in any position, even though he's left-handed."

The veteran Baltimore players liked Ruth's good nature and ribbed him about his childlike antics, dubbing him Dunn's Baby. The nickname was shortened to Babe and soon the entire world would recognize the name, Babe Ruth.

In 1914 a new major league, the Federal League, put a team in Baltimore. The minor league Orioles couldn't compete for attendance with a major league team playing across the street. The Feds offered large salaries to players, and the O's feared Ruth would jump to the

7

St. Mary's Brother Mathias introduced Ruth to baseball. Babe called him "the greatest man I ever met."

Terrapins. Dunn increased Babe's annual salary to $1,800, but when attendance fell, Dunn had to sell his best players. On July 10 he sold pitching ace Ernie Shore, veteran Ben Egan, and Ruth to the Boston Red Sox. Suddenly, Babe was a major leaguer. Although the Federal League folded after two years, it was responsible for Ruth's rapid rise to the big leagues.

The sixth-place Red Sox needed a talent infusion. Boston's three new players arrived at Fenway Park on the morning of July 11, 1914, and manager Bill Carrigan started Ruth on the mound against Cleveland that afternoon. Babe won the game 4 to 3.

Babe's sudden success went to his head. He became cocky, violating the unofficial code of rookie conduct by boasting loudly and going for the fences during batting practice. Just six months earlier he had been a student at St. Mary's. "When they let him out," observed a teammate, "it was like turning a wild animal out of a cage."

"The Red Sox wanted no part of me as a busher," Babe remembered. "Because I liked to hit and took my turn in batting practice with the regulars, I found all my bats sawed in half when I came to my locker the next day."

After he lost two games, the club sent Ruth to their minor league team in Providence, Rhode Island. Back with Boston at the end of the season, he registered his first hit in the majors when he doubled off New York hurler King Cole. Boston finished second behind the A's that year; between Baltimore, Providence, and Boston, Ruth won 24 games.

That first year in Boston was memorable for another reason. When Ruth arrived in the city he had met an attractive sixteen-year-old waitress, Helen Woodford. Two days after the season ended, the couple quietly married. They later adopted a daughter, Dorothy.

In 1915 Babe got off to a strong start with the Sox, launching his first home run on May 6 against the Yankees. Boston went on to capture the American League championship. Ruth finished 18-8 for the season, but he did not get a chance to pitch in the World Series, which Boston won.

Babe's $3,500 salary allowed him to enjoy the big league life. For the first time Ruth had money, but he could not manage it. "He'd buy anything and everything," said Carrigan, the Boston skipper. Carrigan put Ruth on a budget, giving him only a portion of each paycheck and putting the rest aside. At season's end he turned the savings over to his young pitcher. "I calculated it wouldn't last too long, but that was the best I could do."

Babe's lavish spending wasn't Carrigan's only concern. Ruth developed a taste for the nightlife and began breaking curfews during road trips. The manager assigned Babe to hotel rooms next to his own to keep tabs on the wayward young player. Although Ruth occasionally grumbled, he respected Carrigan.

The following season the Red Sox claimed their second consecutive pennant behind Babe's 23 wins. Taking on the Brooklyn Dodgers in the 1916 World Series, Ruth started Game 2 in Boston. He retired the first two hitters, then Hy Myers lined a rope to the right center gap for an inside-the-park home run. Never losing his composure as the afternoon shadows lengthened, Ruth remained on the mound for fourteen innings without surrendering another run in Boston's 2-1 victory. It was the longest game in World Series history.

Even Bill Carrigan, known for his gruff manner, laughed at Babe's postgame clubhouse antics. Like an overgrown kid, the Red Sox ace bounced from locker to locker, embracing everyone in massive bear hugs, including "Rough" Carrigan. "I told you a year ago I could take care of those National League bums," he boasted.

Boston repeated as world champs, taking the 1916 Series in five. Following the Series, Carrigan retired to become a banker. Ruth played for six other major league managers during his long career in baseball, but Carrigan remained his favorite skipper.

On April 6, 1917, the United States entered World War I. Ruth registered for the draft, but continued playing baseball, since single men were called up first. As the season progressed, Babe's personality began to change. The once good-natured Ruth became increasingly irritable and aggressive. Manager Jack Barry was unable to keep Babe reined in, as Carrigan had done.

Babe's new world included pleasures he'd never known. He and Helen traveled in the off-season. He discovered the race track and enjoyed hunting. His weight shot up to 194 pounds, 34 pounds over his rookie year. Teammates weren't surprised. They watched Ruth consume huge quantities of food: steaks or chops with eighteen eggs for breakfast, pounds of raw hamburger or a gallon of ice cream for a snack. As his weight increased, so did his bad temper.

On June 23, 1917, Ruth took the mound at Fenway to face the Senators first hitter, Ray Morgan. Behind the plate stood umpire Brick Owens, who called the first pitch a ball. Ruth objected mildly, but when Owens called his second pitch, "Ball two," Babe yelled and the umpire cautioned him. Owens then pronounced the next pitch "Ball three," and Ruth bellowed, "Open your eyes."

Owens responded by calling out to the mound, "It's too early for you to kick. Get in there and pitch."

Babe reacted like a bull by repeatedly kicking the mound, gouging the soil with his spikes. Finally, he reared back and unleashed his fourth pitch with venom.

"Ball four," rang out Owens.

Ruth headed for the plate. "Why don't you open your . . . eyes."

"Get back out there and pitch," Owens blasted, "or I'll run you out of the game."

"You run me out of the game," Babe yelled, "and I'll punch you in the nose."

"Get . . . out of here!" declared the red-faced ump, signaling Babe to the showers. "You're through."

Catcher Chester Thomas tried to step between Ruth and Owens, but his efforts failed. Babe landed a left on the back of the ump's neck. Two players and a policeman finally pried them apart. American League president Ban Johnson fined Ruth $100 and suspended him for ten days. This would not be the last time Ruth's temper would flare.

Babe ended the year 24-13, but Boston finished 10 games behind the first place White Sox.

In 1918 Ed Barrow took the Red Sox helm. Ruth had become a solid hitter, batting .325 in 1917; 11 of his 40 hits had been for extra bases. The Boston club owner noticed that when Ruth pitched, more tickets were sold. Babe had a reputation as the best left-handed pitcher in baseball, but the club also needed his bat in their daily lineup. On May 6 Barrow started Babe in his first game as an out-fielder. Coming off a 10-game hitting streak, Ruth went hitless, prompting a writer to report, "He didn't hit a thing, not even an umpire."

Babe disliked the gruff Barrow and didn't like playing in the field every day when he wasn't pitching. With little rest, Ruth became tired and he complained to his manager. "Of course you're tired," barked Barrow. "That's because you're running around all the time. If you stopped your carousing at night and took better care of yourself, you could play every day and not feel it."

To add to Babe's problems, as the season neared an end, he received word of his father's sudden death. Apparently, Mr. Ruth and a customer were fighting outside the saloon. The elder Ruth fell, striking his head. At twenty-three, Babe had lost both his parents. Mamie, now married, was the only remaining member of his family.

After being ejected from a game in 1930 by Umpire Brick Owens, Babe yells at the official.

Babe Ruth and Umpires

I called him out on a play, and as he ran by me at first base, he started to give me a little trouble. I told him to get away or I'd chase him. He said, "You umpires don't like me in this league." I said, "Look Babe, I'll give you a tip. We like you. We're just not going to give you anything." (From *The Men In Blue: Conversations with Umpires* by Larry Gerlach, quoting Beans Reardon, umpire)

Despite these setbacks, Ruth had a good season. In addition to winning 13 games against 7 losses, he batted .300 and tied for the league lead with 11 home runs. He led all hitters in slugging percentage, as he would for twelve of the next thirteen years. Once again the Red Sox won the pennant, and took the World Series crown by downing the Chicago Cubs in six games. In his two wins, Ruth ran his World Series record to 29 consecutive shutout innings. For the rest of his life, Ruth treasured this pitching record, which lasted forty-three years, more than all his home run feats.

Tensions mounted between Barrow and Babe as the 1919 season started. The Boston skipper ran a tight ship, enforcing all club rules, especially curfews. When Ruth failed to return to his room until six o'clock one morning, Barrow called a clubhouse meeting before that day's game and blasted Babe's behavior in front of the entire team.

His teammates sat stunned as Ruth's temper exploded. When he threatened to punch Barrow, the manager immediately suspended him for a game. Babe apologized and the two men compromised. Ruth agreed to leave a note in his manager's mailbox stating the time he came in each night. "I never checked up on him again," Barrow later said. "I took his word."

The Babe's performance improved throughout the season. He won 9 games as a pitcher, batted .333 and hit an astounding 29 home runs, more than anyone had hit in one season. He was also the first to hit one homer in every ballpark in the league in one season.

Wherever the Sox played, fans turned out to see Ruth's home runs sail out of the park. It was not only the impressive number of Ruth's homers that was so remarkable, but the way he hit them. His swing featured a distinct upward motion; when the bat connected with the ball, it launched long, arcing home runs that always brought cheers from the delighted fans. Babe's strikeouts were as impressive as his round-trippers, his massive swings slicing through the humid air of summer afternoons across America. "I swing big with everything I've got," he once claimed. "I hit big or I miss big. I like to live as big as I can."

As Ruth rounded the bases following a home run, he was an unforgettable sight for baseball fans lucky enough to see him. His thin legs and small ankles contrasted oddly with the rest of his large body as he trotted pigeon-toed around the diamond.

Babe had brought an immeasurable element of excitement to the game. Other players began asking him for hitting tips. "All I can tell them is pick a good one and sock it. I get back to the dugout and they ask me what it was and I tell them I don't know except it looked good."

Despite Babe's strong showing, the 1919 season ended with the Red Sox in sixth place. Owner Harry Frazee also invested in Broadway shows and needed money for his newest venture. In a shocking move that still haunts Boston fans, Frazee sold Babe Ruth to the rival New York Yankees on December 26, 1919, for $100,000. To this day, the devastating sale of the popular Red Sox star is known in Boston as "the curse of the Bambino." Following Frazee's treasonous act, the Red Sox played in seven World Series, often coming close to victory before a last-minute disaster occurred. Through 1997, they had not won a World Series since Babe pitched them to the 1918 title.

When Babe Ruth arrived in 1920, New York City was home to three major league teams. The National League Giants shared the Polo Grounds with the American League Yankees while the Brooklyn Dodgers, another National franchise, played at Ebbets Field. After just six years in the majors, the twenty-five-year-old Babe had landed in the Big Apple. It would become his town.

The Yankees had struggled since entering the league in 1903. But in 1915 Jacob Ruppert and Tillinghast Huston purchased the franchise, and vowed to make the Yankees contenders. By 1919 the team had climbed to third place. The lineup was beginning to emerge as the original Murderers' Row, a group of famous power hitters.

Babe started the 1920 season in a serious slump. However, on May 1 his dry spell ended when he stepped up to bat at the Polo Grounds against his former BoSox teammates. The Yankees skipper, Miller Huggins, encouraged Ruth, calling out, "Come on, big boy." Loud chatter filled the park, but when Babe connected, everyone heard the unmistakable crack signaling a "Ruthian" homer, and the term entered the language, referring to anything extraordinary. By the end of October, Babe had launched an amazing 54 rockets—more than any other American league *team*—and his slugging average (total bases divided by at-bats) surged to .847, a record no player has ever approached.

From the city's diverse cultural neighborhoods, fans flocked to see Ruth, the Bambino, as some fans called him. Other nicknames formed a growing list. His teammates called him Jidge instead of George. Sportswriters referred to him as the Sultan of Swat, Caliph of Clout, Wali of Wallop, Maharajah of Mash, Behemoth of Bust, Wazir of Wham, and Rajah of Rap. But, with all these tags around his neck, the world knew him simply as the Babe. While the Babe had numerous titles, his memory for other people's names was bad. He called everybody Kid.

Driven by Ruth's bat, the Yankees' attendance soared to 1,289,422, twice the prior year's count and topping the Giants' attendance by 350,000. Led by John McGraw, the game's most famous manager, the Giants had dominated the New York stage, winning six pennants in sixteen years and finishing below second only four times. In that same period, the Yankees had never won a single American League title. Now, by riding Ruth's wave, the tide had turned. Babe later wrote in his autobiography, "Up until I came to New York it was pretty much of a National League town."

The 1921 season signaled the Yankees' arrival as a dominant force in baseball. Ruth hit a record-setting 59 homers, scored 177 runs and drove in 171. Respectful pitchers walked him 144 times. The club not only captured their first pennant, but a twist of fate found them facing the Giants in the first one-ballpark World Series. The Yanks fell to the Giants in eight games, losing the Series 5 to 3. (In the years 1919–1921, the World Series was won on a best-of-nine basis).

In the off-season, players routinely "barnstormed," traveling around the country with a team of major leaguers who played games in cities and towns. Major league rules prohibited World Series players from barnstorming, but just as Ruth ignored other rules, he paid no attention to this one.

When baseball commissioner Judge Landis learned of Babe's violation he suspended Ruth and Bob Meusel, a fellow Yankee, for thirty-nine days of the 1922 season. The Bambino didn't don the pinstriped flannels until May 20, when the Yankees welcomed him back by naming him team captain.

Repeating his prior season's pattern, Ruth started in a slump. Badly overweight and out of shape, he was thrown out at second while attempting to stretch a single into a double. After throwing a handful of dirt in the umpire's face, Babe got his first ejection as a Yankee. Ruth heard a barrage of boos from the fans as he walked to the dugout. When he gave the New York fans a sweeping bow, one man yelled, "You . . . big bum, why don't you play ball?"

In an instant, the Babe's childhood instincts took over. He plunged into the stands after the man, but fans held him back. "Come on down and fight!" he bellowed. "Anyone who wants to fight come down on the field! Aw, you're all alike, you're all yellow."

Afterward, Ruth apologized for throwing dirt in the umpire's face, then told a reporter, "But I did mean to hit that [bum] in the stands. If I make a home run every time I bat, they think I'm alright," he continued. "If I don't they think they can call me anything they like . . . I'll go into the stands again if I have to."

American League president Ban Johnson slapped Babe with a $200 fine and a day's suspension. "Dust on umpires happens in the heat of the moment," Johnson observed, "but we cannot condone anyone going into the stands." However, Ruth's greatest punishment came when the Yankees informed him he was no longer their captain.

Once again the Yankees lost the World Series to the Giants, who swept them in four with one tie. It had been a dismal season for Babe. He batted .315 with 35 home runs; two suspensions and an illness limited him to 110 games.

New York buzzed with gossip about Ruth's eating and drinking too much, partying, and staying out all night. The Babe's earlier remarks about the fans were true. They didn't care about his private life as long as he performed well, but now they felt his bad habits hurt the team.

That winter Ruth attended a dinner in New York where the city's future mayor, James J. Walker, addressed the audience. He openly accused Babe of letting down the "dirty-faced kids" who idolized him. "Are you going to keep on letting those kids down?" Walker asked him.

Stung by Walker's words, Ruth stood up and apologized. "I know as well as anybody else just what mistakes I made last season," he told the audience. "There's no use in me trying to get away from them. But let me tell you something. I want the New York sportswriters and fans to know that I've had my last drink until October. I mean it. Tomorrow I'm going off to my farm. I'm going to work my head off and maybe part of my stomach."

In 1923 the Yankees started the season in their new home, Yankee Stadium, a magnificent facility in the Bronx, across the Harlem River from the Polo Grounds and just a half mile away. True to his word, Babe reported to spring training in good condition, his weight down to 215 pounds. The Yankees opened on April 18 before 74,000 fans who packed the new park and were rewarded with a 4-1 win over the Red Sox. Ruth marked the occasion with a three-run homer that sailed

The Babe connects for one of his four home runs against the Cardinals in the 1926 World Series. He hammered three in a single game.

The Yankees: World Series Kings

From 1926 through 1953, the New York Yankees won 16 of the 17 World Series they played, 6 of them in four-game sweeps. Ruth's greatest Series was 1928 against the Cardinals. He batted .625; of his ten hits in the four games, three were doubles and three were home runs.

Through 1997 the Yankees had won 23 World Series; the St. Louis Cardinals had taken 9, the most won by a National League team.

over the right field wall, the first of 41 he blasted that year. It was also the first home run hit in Yankee Stadium, which became known as "the house that Ruth built."

For the third consecutive year, the Yankees captured the pennant and faced the Giants in the World Series. Unlike the past two seasons, the 1923 Series took place in separate arenas and was dubbed the first "subway series." And unlike other years the Yankees were the victors. Led by Babe's three home runs, the Bronx Bombers claimed their first Series crown, winning four out of six games. The American League's Most Valuable Player award went to Babe Ruth, who had batted a career high .393.

The Bambino led the league in 1924, hitting .378 with 46 homers, but the Washington Senators claimed the pennant. In 1925, a strong young rookie named Lou Gehrig joined the Yankees. Like Babe, Gehrig was of German descent. The two later became friends; Babe often visited the Gehrig home where Lou's mother prepared fine German meals.

Following spring training, the Yankees boarded a New York-bound train, but Ruth never completed the trip. When the train stopped in Asheville, North Carolina, he collapsed on the platform and was taken first to a local hospital, then to New York, where he had surgery. Babe's illness was called "the bellyache heard round the world." When he returned to the team, he played poorly.

Throughout the 1925 season, the Babe broke curfew and manager Miller Huggins was furious with him. During a road trip Huggins hit him with a $5,000 fine and suspended him for disobeying rules on and off the field. When the Babe threatened to punch out his manager, Huggins, fifteen years Ruth's senior, didn't back down. "If I were half your size, I'd punch you," blasted the fiery Huggins, who weighed 100 pounds less and stood six inches shorter than Ruth. "And I'll tell you something else, mister," he continued. "Before you get back in uni-

A smiling Ruth poses with Yankees manager Miller Huggins. Despite Huggins's small size he was clearly the boss, once fining Babe $5,000 for breaking club rules.

form, you're going to apologize for what you've said, and apologize plenty."

Babe later apologized, but Huggins still sat him down for the next nine days. His batting average fell to .290, his home run production to 25. The Yankees finished a dismal seventh and critics predicted the Babe's career was finished. But Ruth proved them wrong with another good year. Fit and trim at the start of 1926 spring training, Ruth rebounded to hit .372 and lead the Yankees back to the top. October found them facing the St. Louis Cardinals in the World Series.

During the season Babe had visited eleven-year-old Johnny Sylvester, a bedridden boy. Ruth promised to send Johnny autographed balls from both teams in the Series and he sent the boy a note: "I'll hit a home run for you in Wednesday's game." Babe belted three home runs that day. Despite Ruth's hot bat, St. Louis took the Series 4 to 3.

When the 1927 season opened, Gehrig and Ruth went head-to-head in home runs. By August 10, Gehrig led 38 to 35, but Babe soon left his teammate in the dust. On September 30 he blasted his 60th shot, a miraculous feat in a memorable year. Many baseball scholars consider the 1927 Yanks the best team in the game's history. As a club they hit .307, winning 110 games with just 44 defeats. They outdistanced the Philadelphia A's by 19 games to claim the pennant and swept the Pirates in the World Series. They also swept the Cardinals in the 1928 Series that ended when Babe made a spectacular catch in the final inning.

While Ruth's career was strong again, his marriage had long since failed. He and Helen had been separated for several years. Their daughter, Dorothy, lived in Massachusetts with her mother. Tragically, Helen died in a fire during the winter of 1929.

As the Yankees began the 1929 season, Babe started a new chapter in his personal life when he married Claire Hodgson on April 17. The couple married at 6:00 A.M. hoping to avoid attention, but when they arrived at the cathedral, thousands waited.

The Yankees began wearing numbers on their uniforms that year. A player's spot in the lineup determined his number. Since Ruth batted third and Gehrig was right behind him, the two became number 3 and number 4, and their numerals became as famous as their names.

From 1929 to 1931 the premier club in the American League was the Philadelphia A's, but the Yankees remained strong with their big guns, Gehrig and Ruth. Babe hit his 500th home run on August 11, 1929, and launched his 600th on August 21, 1931.

While the nation endured the era of financial crisis known as the Great Depression, Ruth's salary climbed to $80,000. His unprecedented earnings raised the standard for all players' salaries. To this day professional baseball players are indebted to the Yankee star for his role in revolutionizing their pay scale.

New York reclaimed the pennant in 1932, sweeping the Cubs in the World Series that featured Babe's "called shot." Ruth, thirty-seven, remained overweight and his knees constantly ached, but despite such problems he hit .341 with 41 roundtrippers for the season.

The first All-Star Game was played at Chicago's Comiskey Park on July 6, 1933. Comiskey's architect had promised, "No player will ever hit a ball out of this park," but Babe, unaware such an impossibility existed, belted a home run over the roof that day.

By 1934 Ruth's popularity had peaked. On July 13 the Sultan of Swat hit his 700th home run at Detroit's Navin Field. Following the season, he joined an All-Star team that toured Japan, where the crowds flocked around Babe, ignoring the other players.

His popularity remained as high as ever, but Babe's career was waning. The excess weight threw off his timing at the plate and his knees were shot; chasing and snagging outfield flies often was impossible. Realizing his playing days were ending, the aging veteran felt the

Ruth's last appearance at Yankee Stadium came in June 1948, when the Yankees retired his number 3. Although he had only two months to live, he left a hospital in July and flew to Baltimore for a charity event. The Babe set 76 records during his career; 62 remained when he died in August 1948.

Yankees owed him a chance to manage the team. When he made his wishes known to Jake Ruppert, the owner's response stung. "How can you manage the team," Ruppert asked, "when you can't even manage yourself?"

Ruth played a risky hand, telling the club he would return only as manager. The Yankees, pleased with skipper Joe McCarthy, offered Babe a job managing their farm team, the Newark Bears, but an insulted Ruth refused. Despite his role with the club as the most important player in the game's history, Babe had placed the Yankees in an impossible situation. They released their aging slugger.

The Babe's excesses and on-the-field temper tantrums now returned to haunt him. Although he felt he'd earned respect, no one viewed Ruth as management material. In desperation, he accepted an offer for the 1935 season to play for the Braves, Boston's floundering National League franchise, when the club hinted at the possibility of a later managerial role.

Before the Babe took off his uniform for the last time, his magic shone for one more brilliant afternoon. On May 25, 1935, at Pittsburgh, he belted three home runs; the final one was the first ball to be hit completely out of Forbes Field. Wild cheers erupted as the Pirates fans stood to applaud the Great Bambino, who had launched his 714th—and last—home run.

A week later, Babe announced his retirement. He hoped for offers to manage a team, but except for a brief stint as a coach with the Brooklyn Dodgers in 1938, no one was interested in him. "Babe would often sit by the phone, waiting for the call that never came," his wife later told an interviewer. "Sometimes when he couldn't take it any longer, he'd break down, put his head in his hands, and cry."

However, Ruth was not forgotten. In 1939, he was honored to be among the first group of players selected for the National Baseball Hall of Fame at Cooperstown. The former stars gathered at the entrance to the museum as the band played "Take Me Out to the Ball Game," and the fans honored Babe with the longest and most affectionate ovation of all. His star still eclipsed all others.

Babe was among the thousands who filled Yankee Stadium on July 4, 1939, to honor Lou Gehrig, his former teammate. Gehrig had become baseball's Iron Horse, playing in 2,130 consecutive games, but his streak ended when he was stricken with a fatal disease. "I couldn't look at him," Babe recalled. "And when he said, 'I consider myself the luckiest man in the world,' I couldn't stand it any longer. I went over to him and put my arm around him, and though I tried to smile and cheer him up, I could not keep from crying."

Eight years later, on April 27, 1947, the cancer-stricken Ruth stood before almost 60,000 fans who had gathered in Yankee Stadium to honor him. He returned to the park a year later for ceremonies commemorating the twenty-fifth anniversary of Yankee Stadium, and the club retired his number 3. As the old-timers gathered for an exhibition game, his old friend Joe Dugan asked Babe how he felt. "Joe, I'm gone," replied Babe as he wept.

Ruth died in New York on August 16, 1948, at age fifty-three. Thousands passed his casket at Yankee Stadium. Countless fathers lifted up their small sons for a final glimpse of the Babe. On August 19, after a requiem Mass at New York's St. Patrick's Cathedral, he was laid to rest in the Gates of Heaven Cemetery in Hawthorne, New York.

Before his death, Babe summed up his life eloquently, telling a writer, "What I am, what I have, what I'm going to leave behind me—all this I owe to the game of baseball."

The Baseball Hall of Fame's first induction ceremony took place in 1939. The ten inductees were, top, left to right, *Honus Wagner, Grover Cleveland Alexander, Tris Speaker, Napoleon Lajoie, George Sisler, Walter Johnson;* bottom, left to right, *Eddie Collins, Ruth, Connie Mack, Cy Young.*

2

A pitcher had to be all but maimed before they took him out.

—Vic Willis

Victor Gazaway "Vic" Willis

Vic Willis's pitching career ended in 1910, long before baseball's Hall of Fame was established, and long before anyone dreamed of counting pitches and using closers. During his thirteen years in the big leagues, Willis started 471 games and finished 388 of them. The right-hander still holds the National League record for most complete games in a season, finishing 45 of his 46 starts in 1902. He worked 410 innings that year, but it didn't ruin his arm. He won 20 or more games in a season eight times; only nine other major league pitchers topped 20 wins more times.

Yet, for all that, Vic Willis remained a forgotten player until one Sunday in July 1995, when he became one of baseball's immortals in Cooperstown, New York.

Victor Gazaway Willis, the son of Joseph T. and Mary Willis, was born April 12, 1876, in Iron Hill Station, a small settlement in Cecil County, Maryland, just west of the Delaware border. His family soon moved across the line to Newark, Delaware, where the brown-eyed, dark-haired Vic grew up. He attended Newark Academy and made the school baseball team. As a teenager, he pitched for Delaware College and earned his first money as a ballplayer pitching for the YMCA for five dollars a game.

He was nineteen in 1895 when he signed with Harrisburg in the Pennsylvania State League as a pitcher/outfielder. At 6 feet, 2 inches and weighing 185 pounds, he was 5-5 in 11 starts and had played right field in 8 games, but his professional debut ended abruptly on June 12 when the club owner couldn't pay his players and disbanded the team.

Willis finished the season with the Lynchburg, Virginia, Hill Climbers, then pitched for the Eastern League's Syracuse Stars in 1896 and 1897. There he caught the attention of scouts with his good control, his sweeping overhand curve, and change-up. Like most big pitchers, he could "deliver the mail," but his most effective pitch was one he dubbed his "grapevine sinker," a drop pitch that acted like today's split-finger fastball.

Syracuse catcher Jack Ryan described the pitch: "Willis's drop is so wonderful that if anyone hits it, it is generally considered a fluke."

After the 1897 season the National League champion Boston Beaneaters bought Willis for $1,000 and catcher Fred Lake. Commenting on the sale, H.G. Merrill of the *Wilkes-Barre Record* noted, "While I am one of the few writers who give the laugh to a chap who talks about strikeout records being a sure criterion of a pitcher's ability, in the case of Willis it is something worth considering, and is a criterion. With the Boston team behind him, Willis ought to be a terror."

Baseball in the 1890s was a different game from the modern version. Grandstands were relatively small, holding about 10,000 fans, but outfields were spacious, sometimes measuring more than 400 feet down the lines and over 500 feet to the center field fence. Games were rarely won with home runs in the twelve-team National League, then the only major league. Batters choked up on the bat and punched the ball through the infield. They relied more on headwork and stealing bases to outscore their opponents. Fielders wore gloves only slightly larger than their hands. Teams had four or five pitchers, who were expected to finish most of what they started and double as relief pitchers when necessary. Most games were played with only one umpire on the field.

Vic Willis made his first major league appearance on April 19, 1898, in Baltimore, when he came in to relieve starter Mike Sullivan with Boston trailing 10 to 3. Nervous, he hit the first two Orioles he faced in the ultimate 18-3 loss.

But the lanky rookie, sometimes called the "tall twirler" by writers, soon gained a spot as a starter, and went on to win 23 games against 12 losses. He completed 29 of his 38 starts, working 311 innings. Looking back on that year, Willis remembered, "I received $1,800 my first season and I really earned it . . . Relief pitchers had not come into style and a pitcher had to be all but maimed before they took him out."

The next year he won 27 and lost 8; writers dubbed him Slick Vic for his talent at "outguessing batters who tried to outguess him." He was second in ERA, fourth in strikeouts, and allowed the fewest hits per game, with five shutouts. A writer for the *Cleveland Plain Dealer* reported, "Willis made the visitors easy mutton for his curves."

In Boston on August 7, 1899, Willis beat Washington 7 to 1 on what everybody in the stands believed was a one-hitter. In the sixth inning,

VICTOR WILLIS.

Willis was twenty-one years old when he won 25 games as a rookie with the Boston Beaneaters in 1898. Teams carried only four or five pitchers in those days; pitchers finished almost every game they started. Portrait sketches appeared regularly in newspapers of Willis's era.

the Washington pitcher, Bill Dinneen, had beat out a dribbler down the third base line for a hit. But the Associated Press reporter gave the third baseman an error on the play and sent out the box score as a no-hitter. So it remains in the record books today as the only no-hitter thrown by Willis.

During this time, Willis met a young woman named Mary Jane Mimmix of Brooklyn. They were married on February 8, 1900. The couple lived in Newark during the winter when Vic wasn't playing ball. They had two children: Gertrude was born in 1900, and Victor Jr. in 1915.

Before the start of the 1900 season, Willis asked Boston for a small raise. He later recalled the fallout. "I came close to being a holdout for 1900 because I had the audacity to ask for a $300 boost on the strength of my work the year before. I got the $2,400, but a player had to be a star to get that much dough in those days when a pitcher was called on every afternoon or so, just to keep him from going stale or loafing."

Willis's contract, which he kept in a safe until he died, called for a $2,100 salary and a $300 bonus if his "conduct, behavior, and playing skill shall be satisfactory during the season."

Despite gaining the raise in pay, Willis had an off-year in 1900, winning only 10 games against 17 losses. He was wild, walking twice as many batters as he fanned.

A baseball war broke out in 1901 when the fledgling American League declared itself a major league and put rival teams in National League cities like Philadelphia, Boston, and Chicago. The Nationals had dropped four of their twelve teams, and the Americans moved into some of those cities, too, offering big salaries to lure National League stars to their new league. The Boston Beaneaters lost several key players, and the team sank in the standings. Both Vic Willis and New York Giants star pitcher Christy Mathewson signed contracts with the new Philadelphia Athletics, but later changed their minds and remained with their old teams.

Willis won 20 in 1901 and 27 in 1902, when he led the league with 225 strikeouts for the only time in his career. After his hard work in the 1902 season, he decided to take the bait of big bucks the American League was still dangling, but he was too late. That winter the warring leagues signed a peace treaty, and Willis had to return to the Beaneaters, who by now were a seventh-place team.

Willis was on hand when tragedy struck in a game at Philadelphia on August 8, 1903. He had pitched a 5-4 twelve-inning win over the Phillies in the first game of a doubleheader.

"I was in the dressing room changing my clothes during the second game," he related, "when I heard a terrible crash. I discovered the overhanging gallery in the left field bleachers had collapsed, carrying with it several hundred fans. Twelve were killed and 282 injured. Police, firemen, and both teams and spectators were helping to extricate those imprisoned in the debris."

The Beaneaters were a disaster as a team. Willis lost 25 games in 1904, when the fielders made 348 errors. "Boston couldn't catch a ball in a peach basket," he later told his grandson. He lost a league-record 29 in 1905, when the team batting average was a meager .234, and the players committed 325 errors.

Then the Pittsburgh Pirates came to his rescue. The Chicago Cubs were the best team in baseball from 1906 through 1910, winning four National League pennants. In 1906 they won 116 games, still the major league record. Their closest rivals were the Pirates and the New York Giants. Both those contenders knew Willis was a better pitcher than his 29 losses indicated. The Pirates won him, trading three players to Boston for the twenty-nine-year-old Delaware Peach.

Willis prospered in Pittsburgh, backed by a supporting cast that included two future Hall of Fame players, shortstop Honus Wagner and

Willis, third from left, back row, *posed with his teammates, the Boston Beaneaters, in 1902.*

The Boston Beaneaters

Although most baseball team names have changed over the past hundred years, a few have stood the test of time: Baltimore Orioles, Chicago White Stockings (later Sox), Detroit Tigers. Many team names reflected the color of the uniform's cap or stockings. Before Vic Willis arrived in Boston, the team was called the Red Caps. But to avoid confusing them with the Cincinnati Red Stockings or Reds, baseball writers began calling them the Beaneaters. The city was famed for its baked beans, a staple of Saturday night suppers. The name was used until 1907.

manager/outfielder Fred Clarke. By mid-1906 he had established himself as the anchor of the staff. The Pittsburgh correspondent for the *Sporting Life* described him:

"There have been events where the opposition punctured his delivery solidly at times, but when the bingles [hits] that count were needed, the men fell, either by a strikeout or pop fly. Willis . . . is the master mind of slab artists [pitchers]. He never pitches a ball without some deep motive. Not a pitch is wasted by this man. Able to deliver a fast and slow ball, it is no wonder that batsmen fail to thwart his plans. Willis can also field his position in a fine manner. You have to beat him to win games."

He won 22 games in 1906, 1907, and 1909; in 1908 he won 23. On June 30, 1909, he pitched the first game in Pittsburgh's new Forbes Field, a 3-2 loss to the Cubs. The modern new ballpark remained the Pirates' home until 1970, when they moved to Three Rivers Stadium.

The Pirates won 110 games in 1909, the second highest total in National League history, and Vic Willis gained his first and only chance to pitch in a World Series. They faced the American League champion Detroit Tigers, led by the game's greatest wizard with a bat and most intimidating base runner, Ty Cobb.

Babe Adams, a twenty-seven-year-old rookie right-hander who had a 12-3 record and 1.11 earned run average during the season, won the opener 4 to 1.

Howie Camnitz, a 25-game winner, started Game 2, but ran into trouble early. With two outs in the top of the third, a bases-loaded single by Detroit's Jim Delahanty (one of five brothers who played in the majors) gave the Tigers a 4-2 lead. With Delahanty on first and the dangerous Ty Cobb on third, Pirates manager Fred Clarke brought in Willis.

As Willis faced the batter, George Moriarty, Cobb danced off third base, then raced for home as the pitch sailed toward the plate. Cobb's

Cartoons appeared frequently on the sports pages during Willis's era and into the 1950s. Willis is pictured "beating" the Phillies.

brilliant slide around catcher George Gibson eluded the tag and he was safe. "That's one thing I'll never forget as long as I live," Willis told an interviewer. "I didn't think Cobb could beat the throw. I often get razzed for letting Ty get away with that theft, but I don't think anybody could have prevented it."

Willis appeared in the Series only once more. He started Game 6, lasted five innings, and took a 5-4 loss. In the seventh game, Babe Adams shut out Detroit 8 to 0, for his third victory. "If it hadn't been for young Babe Adams winning three games for us, I don't think we would have taken that Series," Willis admitted.

The winners' share of $1,825.22 was a welcome bonus on the $4,500 salary Willis earned in each of his four years with the Pirates.

In January 1910, the Pirates sold the thirty-three-year-old Willis to the seventh-place St. Louis Cardinals. He worked only 212 innings, the lowest workload of his thirteen-year career, finishing with a 9-12 record. Following the season, the Cardinals sold him to the Cubs, but with 248 wins (50 of them shutouts) Willis chose to retire. He had saved enough money to fulfill his ambition to own a hotel.

Returning to Newark, he bought the Washington House Hotel on Main Street, where he and his family lived while he served as "room clerk, taproom keeper, and bellhop."

Willis's granddaughter, Marion Hunt, recalled her grandfather taking her to the circus in Wilmington. "He was a quiet man who discussed baseball only when questioned about it," she said. "He also owned a cottage next to the hotel where he and his friends played poker and enjoyed a bowl of his famous turtle soup, which he prepared there. In warmer weather the men played horseshoes outside."

Following a stroke, Vic Willis died on August 3, 1947, at Union Hospital in Elkton, Maryland, not far from his birthplace.

Over the years, as some of Willis's pitching peers were inducted into the Hall of Fame, the Delaware Peach was overlooked. For decades

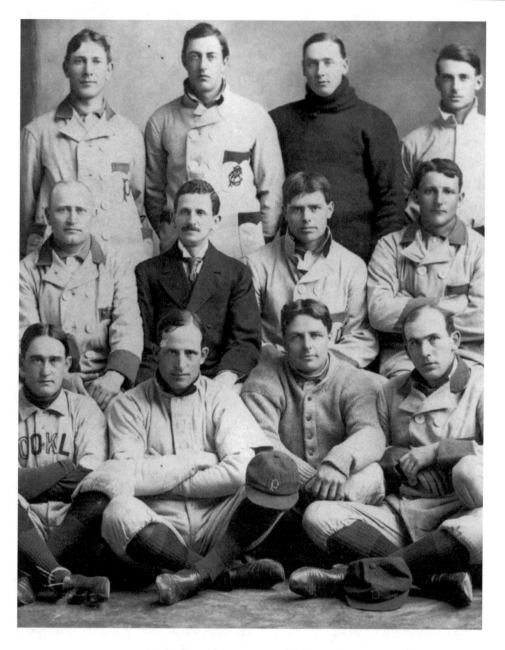

Willis, second from left in back row, *appears with a group of players from different clubs surrounding the Pittsburgh Pirates owner Barney Dreyfuss. The photo shows the various uniform styles worn in the 1910 era.*

his family campaigned for his long overdue recognition. Finally, in 1995, a hundred years after his baseball career began, Vic Willis was voted in by the Veterans Committee of the Hall of Fame.

On July 30, 1995, his grandchildren and great-grandchildren assembled at Cooperstown for the induction ceremony. Great-grandson Thomas Hunt Jr. spoke for the family. "He pitched in a time of baggy pants and no numbers . . . He could throw fast and slow with the same motion, and called his best pitch the grapevine sinker. He put his heart into every game and he prided himself on finishing what he started . . . He was a complete gentleman on and off the field."

3

I dreamed of being a ballplayer even when I was 10 years old working in the fields.

—"Home Run" Baker

John Franklin "Home Run" Baker

In March 1886, baseball's American Association adopted new rules, reducing the number of balls needed for a walk from seven to six, making the pitcher's box one foot deeper, and introducing stolen bases as an official statistic. That same month on the thirteenth, John Franklin Baker was born in a two-story white frame house on his parents' farm near Trappe, a tiny village five miles south of Easton on Maryland's Eastern Shore.

Like most residents of Trappe, Baker's father and grandfather farmed the fertile fields surrounding the community where their English and Scottish ancestors had lived since before the American Revolution. The son of Franklin Adams Baker and Mary Catherine Rust Baker, Frank grew to be a stocky boy who enjoyed helping his father on the farm. When the work was finished he did what all Eastern Shore boys did—he played baseball.

"I dreamed of being a ballplayer even when I was 10 years old working in the fields," Baker once told an interviewer. "I could see myself in a big league uniform. I dreamed of playing before big crowds. I dreamed of being a hero. But never, never, never did I dream that I would ever be in the Hall of Fame."

A sportswriter later wrote, "Frank Baker took to baseball like a Maryland duck to the waters of the Chesapeake." He liked joining the local boys in a game and quickly honed his skills while hitting and playing the outfield.

Frank attributed his athletic ability to his father, describing him as a strong, agile man. "He never saw a trick in the circus he couldn't perform. I saw him one day while he was in his 60s bend over and pick up a 120-pound sack of wheat with his teeth and lift it onto a table. When he was 68 he turned handsprings in the street. He cartwheeled the length of the street in front of our house and finished off by landing on his feet in an upright position."

Frank's older brother, Patsy, was also an excellent baseball player, but Patsy's speed on the base paths was greatly reduced by a childhood accident. One day the boys jumped out of a loft; Frank landed safely, but Patsy broke his leg.

In the early 1900s many Shore towns had semipro ball clubs playing in Saturday and holiday leagues. The players could earn a little cash and scouts were always on hand, bird-dogging for talent for the minor leagues.

In 1905 a scout recommended nineteen-year-old Frank to the Ridgely semipro team's manager, Buck Herzog, a Baltimore native who would reach the majors three years later with the New York Giants. The five dollars Frank earned each game seemed a lot of money to the kid from Trappe. Herzog developed the 5-foot, 11-inch, 175-pound farmboy into a third baseman and remembered him as "the largest and most likable boy in that part of the country."

Baker's heavy arms threw with great speed. His bowed legs resembled those of the famous shortstop, Honus Wagner. Occasionally he looked clumsy scooping up grounders; a writer once described him as "walking like a soft shelled crab."

Baker was playing with the Sparrows Point team near Baltimore in 1907 when he signed with the Eastern League's Baltimore Orioles for a few games at the end of the season. On Saturday, September 14, during the second game of a doubleheader between Baltimore and Rochester at Oriole Park, the O's new manager, Jack Dunn, sent Baker in to pinch-hit in the ninth inning for Charley Schmidt, another local prospect. Baker failed to connect; a Baltimore writer noted the young man from Trappe was "big and strong, but he has not developed the knack of getting his brawn into his swing." Dunn saw no promise in the rookie and let him go, a mistake he soon regretted.

Shirley Povich later wrote in the *Washington Post,* "Frank Baker was the cross the late Jack Dunn of the Baltimore Orioles bore during most of his career. Dunn, the great prospector for talent, who divined greatness in such youngsters as Lefty Grove, George Earnshaw, Joe Boley, and Max Bishop, fluffed miserably the chance to sign a boy from the Eastern Shore by the name of J. Franklin Baker . . . Dunn, unimpressed by the gawky country kid, sent him home."

The following season, Baker played third for the Reading, Pennsylvania, team in the Tri-State League. His .300 batting average and six home runs made an impression on Philadelphia Athletics manager

Connie Mack, who brought him up for the final eight games of the 1908 season. "It was either the 18th or 20th of September when I joined the A's," Baker later remembered. "Mr. Mack was in the (hotel) dining room and I went up to him and said, 'Well, here I am.'

"He looked at me and said, 'I see you are.'"

The A's opened the 1909 season on April 12 in their magnificent new home, Shibe Park, a modern steel-and-concrete facility where 31,160 fans looked on. Baker had been spiked by Sherry Magee in a preseason game against the Phillies and could not play for the first twelve days. He started his first game on April 24. Coming to bat in the first inning with the bases loaded, the twenty-three-year-old Baker hit a home run. "My first home run in the majors was what they now call 'a grand slam,'" he recalled. "We had men on second and third and the Boston pitcher was a fellow named Fran Arellanes. He walked Danny Murphy to get at me.

"When Murphy got down to first base, he said to Jake Stahl, 'That was a mistake walking me. That kid can hit the ball outta the park.'

"And on the first pitch to me I hit it over the right field fence. When I got back to the bench Murphy said, 'Kid, you made Jake Stahl think I am the greatest prophet in baseball.'"

Later that season, Baker was involved in a spiking incident with the hard-playing Ty Cobb that quickly mushroomed in the press reports. The A's and Tigers were locked in a battle for first place in the American League when the Tigers swept a crucial series from the A's at Detroit's Bennett Park on August 24, 25, and 26. During the first game, Cobb sprinted from first on a single, sliding with upturned spikes as Baker guarded third. Cobb's cleats opened a small wound on Baker's arm and blood flowed, prompting accusations of foul play. The gash required ten stitches, but Baker finished the game; he didn't miss any playing time as a result of the injury, but A's fans were livid. The writers' dramatic depiction of the event fueled the tension.

Philadelphia fans attacked Cobb with threatening letters, and when the Tigers visited Philly, Cobb's security detail rivaled the president's. Sportswriter Fred Lieb reported, "His (Cobb's) automobile was surrounded by a platoon of motorcycle police, and between him and the crowd in right field at Shibe Park was a solid wall of Billy Penn's faithful bluecoats."

The A's mounted a late season charge against the Tigers, spurred by the bats of Baker and outfielder Danny Murphy. But Detroit finished three games ahead of Philadelphia to win the pennant. Despite his disappointment, Connie Mack had to be pleased with his Eastern Shore rookie, who batted .305 in 148 games.

In 1910 Baker hit a respectable .283 with two home runs as the A's finally captured the pennant and faced the Chicago Cubs in the World Series. Philadelphia defeated Chicago 4 to 1 in the first game behind Baker's single, two doubles, and two RBI. The A's went on to win the Series 4 games to 1, with Baker hitting .409.

The 1910 season marked the final year of the dead ball era. With the introduction of the lively new cork-centered ball, batting averages rose sharply the following year.

In 1911 Connie Mack added first baseman John Phalen "Stuffy" McIinnis to the A's infield of Eddie Collins at second, Baker at third, and Jack Barry at shortstop, creating an offensive and defensive squad unequaled in baseball. Connie Mack encouraged the quartet to create their own plays. They invented strategies to foil sacrifice bunts and the double and triple steals widely used at the time.

The *Sporting News* reported that a writer once asked Mr. Mack if he would take $100,000 for his talented infield. (In 1911, $100,000 was the equivalent of $100 million today.) "I wouldn't take $100,000 for my infield," he replied. The story circulated in Philadelphia and Baker, Barry, Collins, and McInnis would be forever known as the $100,000 infield.

Baker led the American League in home runs in 1911, 1912, 1913, and 1914, but never hit more than 12 in a season.

The Dead Ball Era

Although twelve seems a low number by today's standards, home runs were harder to hit when Home Run Baker played. The same ball would be used for several innings, no matter how dark or mushy or lopsided it became. Fans were required to return foul balls that were hit into the stands so they could be put back into play. Playing fields were more expansive than they are today; most home runs were inside-the-park.

Baker and the A's performed brilliantly throughout 1911, easily clinching the American League Championship. Bake, as he was called by his teammates, ended the regular season batting .334 with a league-leading 11 home runs.

The 1911 World Series promised to be a classic contest as the A's took on the New York Giants, skippered by John McGraw. The Giants won the first game on their home turf at the Polo Grounds and faced Philadelphia at Shibe Park two days later on October 16. In the sixth inning, Baker stepped up to the plate with the game tied at 1 to 1. New York's Rube Marquard, another Maryland native, delivered a high fastball to Baker, who crushed it over the fence. The A's and their southpaw, Eddie Plank, held the lead to win 3 to 1.

For that series the two teams moved back and forth daily between the opposing clubs' ballparks. Following the Philadelphia game, the teams traveled the short distance back to New York for Game 3 at the Polo Grounds the next day.

In those days sports journalists often wrote stories that appeared in magazines and newspapers under a player's byline. After the Giants' loss to the A's in Philadelphia, a story appeared in a New York paper written by such a ghostwriter for New York's pitching ace, Christy Mathewson. The writer, using Mathewson's name, criticized Marquard's pitch selection by stating, "Everyone knows Baker can't hit a low curve."

On October 17 Mathewson took the mound for the Giants against the A's Jack Coombs. The Giants hurler blanked the A's for eight innings and led 1 to 0 when Baker faced him with two outs in the ninth. "Matty had that wonderful fadeaway—the pitch they now call a screwball," Baker later remembered. "He got two strikes on me and instead of throwing the fadeaway he tried a low, outside curve ball. And I hit that one over the right field fence. The very pitch he thought Marquard should have thrown to me."

Baker's last-minute heroics tied the game, sending it into extra innings. The A's scored twice in the eleventh inning. New York mounted a comeback, but their effort fell short and Philadelphia won 3 to 2.

Rain pelted the east coast for the next six days; it was October 24 before the two teams resumed play in Philadelphia. The A's beat New York 4 to 2 behind the bats of Baker, Barry, and Murphy, who each pounded two doubles.

After the Giants won the fifth game 4 to 3 in ten innings, they returned to Shibe Park on October 26. The A's won their second consecutive World Series before the hometown crowd, soundly trouncing New York 13 to 2. (It remained the World Series' latest ending date until 1989, when a California earthquake suspended play.)

Baker hit .375 for the Series. His two dramatic home runs earned him the nickname Home Run Baker, and it stuck.

Baker undoubtedly benefited from the corked ball in 1911, but he had also improved his hitting skills since entering the majors. Like all great sluggers, he did not press at the plate and had a "good eye." Years after his memorable first home run in the majors, he described his hitting theory. "I was pretty husky, but there was something else. When I swung at a ball I knew it was where I wanted it to be. I waited until the last split-second before I swung. I wasn't one of those fellows who was always 'way out in front of the ball . . . I never took any signs on pitched balls. I always waited to look at that ball—never trusted a tip."

Baker's punch at the plate was all the more remarkable because pitchers regularly doctored the ball. "I'd like to see them (today's players) swinging against the spitters, shiners, and emery balls at which we used to look. About the worst of all was the 'dark' ball. Following a couple of trips around the infield, smacked into gloves floating in tobacco juice, a new ball would be as black as a black hat. Such a ball thrown by a pitcher like Walter Johnson was almost impossible to see. I've swung with all my might at a good fast ball, hit it fair and square and was lucky if it bounced against the fence. I hit the fence in Shibe Park 38 times in one year. Eddie Collins told me if I had been hitting the ball Babe Ruth hit every one of them would have gone over the fence."

When Baker stepped up to the plate he carried a piece of lumber packing punch. "I used a man-sized bat," he explained. "Up until I got too old to get around on good fast ball pitching, I used a 52-ounce bat. You had to hit that ball fair and square and with some weight and power back of it to make it go over the fence."

Jack McGrath of the Louisville Slugger Company reported, "Baker used a bat antiquated even in his time. It was short, but almost like a piece of lead because it weighed 52 ounces . . . it really was a wagon-tongue. There was no flex . . . the handle was almost as round as the barrel."

In 1912 Baker belted 10 more home runs and batted .347 with a slugging average of .541. The A's finished second to the Red Sox that year, but Philadelphia rebounded the following season to again fly the American League flag over Shibe Park.

Along with his superb hitting skills, Bake was no slouch on the base paths. "I could get a longer lead off second, plus a better study of the pitcher," he told an interviewer. "Quick starts were generally responsible for the many bases I was able to steal, particularly in 1912. George Mullin, a Detroit right-hander, was the toughest pitcher to steal on. He pitched with a leaning motion which made it practically impossible to take a lead off first. I distinctly remember that the A's had at least a dozen men caught off the bag by his "balk motion" as we called it.

"After much study I learned that some pitchers had a slight leaning motion that tipped off the runner when they were going to make a play," he explained. "However, I don't recall any of the truly great pitchers having any giveaway signs. I stole third more times than I was able to swipe second. From second, I could detect any flaw in the pitcher's motion."

The three sluggers from the 1921 Yankees original Murderers' Row are, from left, Babe Ruth, Frank Baker, and Bob Meusel. That year Ruth's total of 59 home runs was more than double runnerup Meusel's production of 24. After winning their first pennant in 1921, the Yankees won five more in the next seven years.

During the 1913 season, Bake hit .336 and a career-high 12 home runs, which led the American League. On October 7, he and his teammates met the Giants once more at the Polo Grounds in the World Series opener. Baker's three RBI and his fifth-inning home run lifted Philadelphia to a 6-4 victory. The A's went on to take the Series 4 games to 1."It was Baker's peculiar good fortune to have his 14 base blows come at a particular time when they counted," observed John J. Ward in *Baseball Magazine.* "As a home run pinch hitter, if we may use that term, he has had no equal in World Series history."

On March 25, 1914, the A's met the Baltimore Orioles for an exhibition game in Fayetteville, North Carolina, the O's spring training home. As Baker stepped into the batter's box, he faced a left-handed Baltimore rookie named George Ruth, who pitched his team to a 6-2 win. But Baker connected off the young southpaw from St. Mary's Industrial School for a double and three singles.

That year, Connie Mack's A's earned their fourth trip to the fall classic in five seasons after easily capturing the American League pennant by 8 games. But Philadelphia fell in 4 straight games to the Boston Braves in the first World Series sweep.

Baker's .250 average with 4 hits during the Series contributed to the club's loss, but his regular season performance had been strong, as he hit .319 and added 9 home runs next to his name.

Despite another pennant-winning season, Philadelphia fans failed to support the A's throughout 1914. Connie Mack speculated that fans became complacent whenever there was no close pennant race. There were other factors. Americans now had a variety of entertainment activities to choose from: amateur and semipro baseball games, golf, and movies. Many people bought and enjoyed automobiles. Major league baseball had to compete for a share of the recreation budget.

In addition, a mood of concern had swept over much of the nation during that summer as Americans increasingly heard about the growing war in Europe. It seemed the United States might be drawn into the war. Every American League team lost money that year.

Connie Mack faced another monumental problem. The rival Federal League was organizing teams in several cities. The well-financed Feds offered big salaries to lure players away from the National and American Leagues. The stars on the A's winning team required a huge payroll. Mack could not match the new league's offers and he lost pitchers Eddie Plank and Chief Bender to the Feds. Expecting to lose Jack Coombs as well, Mack let the pitcher go to the Brooklyn Dodgers. Unable to meet the Feds' offer to Eddie Collins, he sold the second baseman to the White Sox for $50,000. Philadelphia's $100,000 infield was no more.

Mack had signed Baker to a three-year contract to keep his star third baseman away from the Feds, but Baker was getting tired of the travel and thought he might want to stay home with his wife and two daughters and work on the farm. He also believed that Mr. Mack should give him a raise despite their multiyear agreement. "Every man has the price at which he is willing to work. I have mine," Baker told a writer. "I am not stating what it is, but I will take it if it is offered."

It was not the first time Baker had made such comments to his manager during contract negotiations, but now Connie Mack was in no mood to listen. Equally stubborn, the two men cut off communications. True to his word, Frank "Home Run" Baker, one of the most valuable players in baseball, sat out the 1915 season, playing with a semipro team in Upland, Pennsylvania.

Stripped of much of their talent, the A's plunged to the American League cellar, a spot they occupied for the next six years before finishing seventh in 1922.

Now unable to afford Baker at any price, and believing the third baseman would not be happy returning to the A's, Connie Mack sold him to the New York Yankees on February 15, 1916, for $35,000.

51

The Yankees did not own their own ballpark when Baker joined the club. Instead, they rented the Giants' home, the Polo Grounds. The two clubs were able to share the park, as one was always on the road when the other was at home.

Baker started off well with New York, but going after a foul fly, he crashed into an open gate at the Polo Grounds and cracked several ribs. It idled him for 50 games and cost him another home run crown. He hit 10 homers in 100 games, but his teammate, first baseman Wally Pipp, led the league with 12. Baker's hitting and home run production fell during the next three years. "I broke three ribs among other things and battered myself up so much that I have never been able to swing as freely at the ball or with such force as I used to," he explained.

Baker missed the 1920 season when personal tragedy struck. His wife died, and he stayed home with his two young daughters until his sister and her husband moved in to care for the children.

Returning to the Yankees in 1921, Baker started spring training with a new teammate named Babe Ruth, who had joined the club the prior year. "He can hit the ball farther than anybody I ever saw," Baker later said. "There has never been anybody like him and I don't believe there ever will be anybody like him."

Baker's hopes of starting the season with a strong performance were soon dashed when, making a quick start to field a ball, he tore a muscle in his knee, forcing him to become a part-time third baseman. He still batted .294 in the first Murderers' Row, a lineup of sluggers that included Babe Ruth, Wally Pipp, Roger Peckinpaugh, and Bob Meusel. Behind their big bats, New York captured their first pennant, facing the crosstown Giants in the first one-city World Series since 1906. New York City exploded with excitement as the two teams met in their Polo Grounds home where the Yanks fell to the Giants in 8 games (from 1919 to 1921 the World Series was a five-out-of-nine contest).

In the late 1930s Frank Baker, right, is visited by fellow big leaguers Jimmie Foxx, left, and Eddie Collins in Easton. All three played for the Philadelphia Athletics; Baker and Collins formed half of the famed $100,000 infield of the 1910–1914 era. Second baseman Collins was among the first group inducted into Baseball's Hall of Fame in 1939 with Baltimore's Babe Ruth.

In 1922 the thirty-six-year-old Baker repeated his part-time role at third and hit .278, but his injuries had taken a toll. His last appearance in big league baseball was as a pinch-hitter in the 1922 World Series, which the Yankees again lost to the Giants.

The veteran slugger retired with a career batting average of .307 over fifteen years. Baker had led the American League in home runs four times and RBI twice. He batted .363 in six World Series.

Baker returned to his home and two daughters in Trappe, where he managed the Easton team in the Eastern Shore League and enjoyed farming, hunting, and raising bird dogs. He eventually remarried; he and his second wife, Margaret, had a son and a daughter.

In January 1955, Home Run Baker was elected to the Hall of Fame and was inducted with Joe DiMaggio, Dazzy Vance, Ted Lyons, and Gabby Hartnett in ceremonies on July 25. "This is something— you can't find words to express what's in your heart," said Baker.

Baker's love of the game remained strong. "Baseball just is a different game today than when I played," he observed. "Our game was good and fun to play. Home runs were much rarer, but I used to get a big bang out of hitting one, and so did the Philadelphia fans. Now they hit as many home runs in a day as we sometimes hit in a month, but the present game is a good spectacle, and the crowds certainly do enjoy it."

The veteran slugger faithfully attended the old-timers games in Philadelphia and New York until poor health prevented him. At seventy-seven, he suffered a stroke at his home in Trappe, where he died on June 29, 1963.

J. Frank "Home Run" Baker left his mark on the national pastime. Just two years before his death he said, "Baseball is a grand game. The older I get, the crazier I am about it. There's nothing finer."

Seated in the center of the 1924 Easton team is manager Frank "Home Run" Baker, who signed Jimmie Foxx, back row center, *to his first professional contract.*

4

I guess I'll die with a baseball in my hand. I just love the game.

—Judy Johnson

William Julius "Judy" Johnson

The first frosts blanketed the fields bordering Snow Hill, Maryland, on October 26, 1899, when William Henry Johnson and Annie Lee Johnson welcomed the birth of their first son, William Julius.

The Civil War had ended thirty-four years earlier in 1865, but strict segregation laws still existed throughout the South and in the border state of Maryland. Known as Jim Crow laws, they required that African Americans live apart from whites, and their children attend separate schools.

These schools were often housed in second-rate buildings and equipped with cast-off furniture and used books handed down from white schools. Many black children dropped out of school to work in the fields. Despite the existence of a private college for black students in nearby Princess Anne (known today as the University of Maryland, Eastern Shore Campus), few locals attended.

In Maryland's rural areas, African Americans lived in their own communities, attended their own churches, and had little contact with whites except through their jobs as domestic workers and farm laborers. Black people also had limited recreational opportunities; Jim Crow laws forbade them from using facilities that traditionally catered to whites, such as ball parks, pool halls, and bowling alleys.

Records show the existence of professional and semiprofessional baseball teams for black players as far back as 1862. These teams were loosely organized, with clubs starting and disbanding frequently until 1920, when the first lasting Negro League was formed. Small communities such as Snow Hill continued to field local teams.

Johnson's hometown, named for the Snow Hill section of London, was an agricultural community situated on the Pocomoke River on the lower Eastern Shore. At the turn of the century, it was a thriving port surrounded by farms that produced tomatoes, corn, and wheat. Jobs were available, but many black people chose to move to urban areas that offered more employment opportunities and better pay. Cities such as Washington, Baltimore, and Wilmington, Delaware, attracted a large influx of black families.

While he was still in elementary school, young William's family moved to Wilmington, where they eventually settled at 5th and Scott Streets. A baseball park bordered the Johnsons' backyard but before William and his friends could play ball, they had to clean up after the cows and horses that grazed in the field. "Every chance I got I was on that field. I was morning, noon, and night playing baseball," he told an interviewer. "In those days kids always had chores to do at home, chopping kindling wood, beating the rugs, sweeping. There was always work to do. I did my chores real fast so I could get out to the ball field."

The field at DuPont and 2nd Streets became a baseball mecca. So many children came to the diamond that they had to take turns playing. "A lot of Italian kids and kids from Defiance (another neighborhood) would come to play," Johnson later recalled. "We had so many kids wanting to play the most you could get to play was an inning or two. A lot of people used to come out to watch. They would sit on orange crates and peach baskets and we'd pass the hat and collect some coins."

Like kids across America, William and his friends were always in need of baseballs. "When we played regular teams each team would pitch in a ball. The winning team would get to keep both balls," he explained. "We used to pay a quarter for game balls and used taped balls for practice. When we played away games in other parts of Wilmington, we'd walk, carrying all our equipment. We didn't have the nickel for trolley fare."

William's father worked at DuPont's Deepwater plant, but his interest in fitness and boxing prompted him to become a licensed boxing coach. The elder Johnson turned his family's backyard into a neighborhood gym where children could use the monkey bars, bar bells, punching bags, and a trapeze. "My Daddy liked physical fitness and wanted me to be a prizefighter," Johnson remembered.

But it was William's sister Emma who inherited her father's boxing skills, acting as her kid brother's instructor and sparring partner. Later, Johnson enjoyed telling visitors about sparring with his sister. "Those old gloves (boxing) were stuffed with horsehair and were as hard as a brick. My daddy warned me not to hit her in the face or the stomach. But I didn't have much chance to hit her. It was all I could do to avoid her haymaker [a knockout punch]. One day one of her gloves flew off. When she stooped to pick it up—" Johnson paused and smiled at his visitor as if to say, "You know what happened." That was the end of the boxing lessons.

Eventually, Mr. Johnson became the athletic director of the city's Negro Settlement House that provided recreational activities for children. On weekends, he played on the Royal Blues, a city baseball team, and his son became the Blues' batboy. William's greatest ambition was to play baseball. He never forgot joining an organized youth team and getting his first baseball uniform, telling author John Holway, "I was (dressed and) strutting around at 5:00 A.M. The game didn't start until 2:00 P.M."

With little money for equipment, William used his father's old glove, even though the decaying leather was crumbling like dry clay. His first spikes were fashioned by a shoemaker after the boy took him a pair of shoes and metal cleats. But William forgot to remove the heels from the shoes before taking them to the shoemaker, so the spikes tipped him forward in an awkward stance.

Baseball provided the boy's first paying job as a scorekeeper for a local league with several teams. Allowed to leave school five minutes early on game days, he rushed to the park to collect his ten-cent salary before the game. Then he'd spend half his earnings on a fish cake sandwich, savoring every morsel before his official scorekeeping duties began.

Johnson attended Howard High School, which was then located at 12th and Orange Streets. "It was quite a walk, but my mother wouldn't let us leave the house until the last possible minute," he remembered. "She figured that way we wouldn't have time to fool around on the streets."

William played on the school baseball team, but he dropped out in his second year "because my people were so poor I couldn't get decent clothes to go to school." He worked as a stevedore on the docks during

World War I, but in his spare time he could be found on the city sand-lots, playing shortstop or third base on teams all over town.

William played both baseball and football on the St. Thomas Church teams. "I was the first Negro to play on a white football team at St. Thomas," Johnson remembered. "I was a halfback and a drop kicker. I could really kick that ball." St. Thomas's baseball club was a semipro team, and William claimed he was the first black man to play on a white semipro team in Wilmington.

Eventually he landed with the local Rosedale club and struck up a friendship with the team's captain. William frequently visited his new friend's home after games, supposedly to talk baseball. But it was no coincidence that the captain's pretty sister, Anita T. Irons, a school teacher, happened to be home during such baseball chats. Soon William and Anita were courting. They were married on December 27, 1923, and the marriage spanned sixty-three years, ending with Anita's death in 1986. The couple adopted a daughter, Loretta.

When the country entered World War I in April 1917, many baseball clubs lost players to the armed services and had to hire replacements. Johnson signed on with his first professional team, the Giants, for a game in nearby Chester. The following year he tried out for the top local professional club, the Hilldales, in Darby, Pennsylvania. However, the 5-foot, 11-inch infielder weighed only 145 pounds. The Hilldales thought he was too small and sent him home.

Johnson honed his skills by playing with the local Chester Stars in 1920 before signing with Philadelphia's semipro Madison Stars the following year. By then, the young player had added 10 pounds to his frame, but he remained slim the rest of his career, never weighing over 155 pounds.

At Madison, Johnson acquired the nickname Judy. "Madison previously had an old-time first baseman named Robert Jude (pronounced Judy) Gans," Johnson explained. "Someone said, 'You look enough like Judy Gans to be his son.' So they called me Judy and the name stayed with me."

In 1921 Johnson got his big break when the Hilldales called him up in midseason. The rookie earned $115 a month, plus meal money of fifty cents a day and a dollar on Sundays, when they played doubleheaders. He hit a modest .227, but the team won their championship and met the American League Giants in a playoff. In Game 3, Johnson tripled and hit a home run, helping the Hilldales to a 15-5 win.

The following season, Bill Francis became the Hilldales player-manager and he made Judy his starting shortstop. When Frank Warfield took the helm later that season, he moved Johnson back to the hot corner, where he would remain as the Hilldales starting third baseman for the next seven years.

To earn extra money, Negro Leagues teams played exhibition games against white teams before and after the regular season. Johnson tasted danger for the first time while playing such a game in northeast Pennsylvania's coal mining region. The home plate umpire also happened to be the local sheriff. When all his calls went in favor of the home team, the Hilldales took action. Catcher Louis Santop went out to the mound and told the pitcher to throw a hard one that he would let go by so it would hit the ump. The pitcher fired one in. Santop made no effort to catch it. The ball hit the ump in the groin. As he doubled over in agony, the Hilldales raced to their cars. "They chased us six miles down the road. I was really scared," Johnson recalled.

On one 880-mile nonstop bus trip between Chicago and Philadelphia following a doubleheader, the team survived on sandwiches, sodas, and a few naps. When the bus finally reached its destination, Johnson's ankles had ballooned to twice their normal size. Despite the swelling, he played third base in another doubleheader.

In 1923 John Henry "Pop" Lloyd joined the club as a player-manager. Johnson later explained Lloyd's importance in his career.

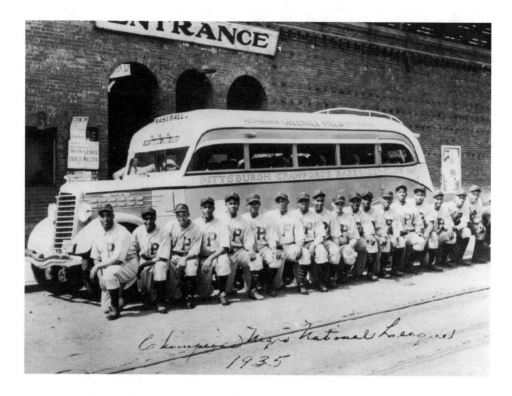

Negro Leagues teams traveled in cars and buses, sometimes driving hundreds of miles to play games in different cities on the same day. Judy Johnson, eighth from right, *is pictured with the 1935 Negro Leagues Champion Pittsburgh Crawfords.*

The Pittsburgh Crawfords

The Pittsburgh Crawfords came into being in the 1920s. They were named after the Crawford Bath House on Crawford Avenue in Pittsburgh's black area. They were a local amateur team. . . . The Crawfords became professional in 1930, after Gus Greenlee, a local numbers (illegal lottery) king, took over the ownership. Greenlee's goal was to surpass the Homestead Grays as Pittsburgh's best team, and he would succeed for a time. (From *The Negro Leagues Book,* edited by Dick Clark and Larry Lester)

"He's the man I gave the credit to for polishing my skills. He taught me how to play third and how to protect myself. John taught me more than anyone else."

Lloyd taught Judy all the angles it took to win, including how to decoy base runners. "I'd act as if the ball wasn't coming and then tag 'em when they came in standing up. They'd call you a lot of bad names . . . This was our game—run, steal, make them make some bad mistakes."

Johnson became a shrewd student of the game. Although he was not quick on the base paths, he observed pitchers until he knew their every move and turned their habits into opportunities to steal second or third. Judy also learned to "kick the sack," quickly and lightly touching the base with his toe following a catch while firing the ball to first for a double play.

In 1920 Chicago American Giants owner Andrew "Rube" Foster, along with owners of other black professional teams, had formed the first Negro National League. Foster, a former ace pitcher in the Negro Leagues, was determined to organize a lasting league with financial stability. Following Foster's example, the Eastern Colored League was organized in 1923 and included the Hilldales as well as teams from Atlantic City, Baltimore, Brooklyn, and New York. Later, others joined, including clubs from Washington and Harrisburg, and the Homestead Grays from Pittsburgh.

Lloyd led the Hilldales to their first Eastern Colored League pennant in 1923. Johnson finished the season hitting a solid .391. The Hilldales captured their second consecutive pennant in 1924 and faced the Kansas City Monarchs in the first official Colored World Series. Johnson led all batters, hitting .364 with five doubles and a triple. He also led in RBI (8) and hits (16), and sweetened those numbers with an inside-the-park home run. But the Hilldales lost the historic nine-game series.

In 1925 Johnson continued to put up big numbers, hitting .364. The Hilldales clinched their third pennant and captured the Colored World Series in 6 games.

During this era Johnson noticed offensive play growing more aggressive. As competition intensified, players used any tactic to gain an edge over an opponent; intimidation was a normal part of a player's weaponry. Some carried small handbags to hide metal files for sharpening spikes.

Pop Lloyd taught Johnson many protective strategies, including wearing shinguards. Johnson still received numerous scars. "Mother never wanted to see me play," he said. "The only time she saw me play, we were playing in Darby, Pennsylvania, against Earle Mack's All-Stars. This boy named Red Padgett from the Cleveland Indians was stealing third. I'd always put my foot down and block them. When Padgett slid in, he scraped my foot with those big league spikes of his, right through to a corn on my little toe. I went down howling and struggling to get my shoe off. My mother must have thought I'd had my leg amputated." Mrs. Johnson fainted in the stands and never watched her son play ball again.

When Johnson played winter ball in Cuba, he sometimes roomed with shortstop Dick Lundy of the Bacharach Giants. But that friendship didn't matter during the regular season. One day Lundy slid into third as Judy took the throw. Lundy's spikes ripped open the third baseman's arm.

"Hey," Johnson objected. "I'm your roommate."

"We're playing baseball now," snapped Lundy. "Get out of my way."

Johnson promised himself to repay Lundy at the first opportunity. Seizing a chance to steal second, he plowed into the base as Lundy ran over to cover the bag. "I was waiting for him to come down to tag me," Judy is quoted by author John Holway. "I was going to cut him in half. But when I let out to hit him, he hit me up side the head with the ball. I was going through the air, and he just popped me right side of the head. He just blinded me."

In August 1926, Johnson was beaned during a game at Atlantic City and for the next two seasons his batting average dropped as he struggled to regain his confidence. He bounced back in 1929, hitting a career-high .390. Sportswriter Rollo Wilson of the *Pittsburgh Courier* named Judy Johnson the league's Most Valuable Player that year. "If you'd ever seen him play and marked his pep and ability," wrote Wilson, "you'd know why I chose him over all the rest."

Lloyd Thompson, former Hilldales scorekeeper and writer, also praised Johnson. "Judy could do all that is required to make up a sterling third baseman and do it better than the rest of the field. A right-handed hitter, Judy developed a peculiar stance at the plate and hit the ball hard to all corners of the lot. Slight of build, this Hilldale luminary was a fielding gem, whose breathtaking plays on bunts and hard smashes are treasured among many fans' memories."

Johnson was also a shrewd hitter who practiced a scientific approach to hitting. Despite his slight build, he carried a 40-ounce bat. He never swung for the fences, but used a short stroke and wrist action to spray line drives to all fields.

Johnson became known as the black Pie Traynor, because his playing style and offensive skills mirrored those of Traynor, the Pittsburgh Pirates Hall of Fame third baseman. Later, when asked if it would be correct to compare him with Pie Traynor and Brooks Robinson, the elderly Johnson replied, "I don't know, but it's just good to be mentioned in the same breath with them."

As Judy's best season ended, the stock market crashed on October 29, 1929, beginning the Great Depression. Ticket sales plummeted and the Eastern Colored League folded in 1930.

In Pittsburgh, two teams were able to maintain financial stability even after the depression began. The owners of the Pittsburgh Crawfords

Not only was Judy Johnson an outstanding third baseman, he was solid offensively. He hit an estimated .406 in 1929 with Philadelphia's Hilldales. Negro Leagues statistics are incomplete; not every game was reported in newspapers, and box scores were often omitted. Teams kept their own records.

and the Homestead Grays were also involved in gambling operations. The profits from these illegal activities subsidized their teams during the country's growing financial crisis. These teams played night games before major league fields had installed lights, using portable generators and light poles that were little brighter than candles.

Johnson joined the Homestead Grays as a player-coach in 1930, earning the largest salary of his career. The club boasted one of the hottest lineups in the Negro Leagues with stars such as Oscar Charleston, Buck Ewing, and Smokey Joe Williams.

One night the Grays catcher, Buck Ewing, split a finger. Sitting in the stands was a teenage catcher, Josh Gibson. Some of the Grays had seen Gibson play, and they called him down from the stands to take Ewing's place. Gibson stayed with the team and became the Negro Leagues' greatest slugger.

Johnson didn't hesitate to use a little psychology now and then. One day Satchel Paige was pitching for the Grays against the Philadelphia Stars before a big crowd at Yankee Stadium. It was a close game. The Stars had the bases loaded with none out in the ninth. Johnson called time and walked to the mound. He told Paige that the Stars had been boasting about how they were going to embarrass him in the game. It was a lie, but Paige believed him, and, fired up, he fanned the next three batters on nine pitches.

In 1931 Judy hooked up with the Darby Daisies, a spin-off of the Hilldales. By 1932 he bounced back to the Grays, but the club's owner, Cum Posey, was having financial problems, so Johnson jumped to the crosstown rival Crawfords, owned by the wealthy Gus Greenlee.

Over the next few seasons Greenlee raided the Grays, acquiring the team's most talented players. By 1935, the Crawfords lineup, managed by Oscar Charleston, included Judy Johnson, Satchel Paige, Josh Gibson, and Cool Papa Bell. These hitters posed a formidable challenge to

Judy Johnson's career ended after he played for the Negro Leagues Pittsburgh Crawfords in 1936, eleven years before the major leagues were integrated.

the best pitchers and were compared to the New York Yankees Murderers' Row.

At the end of the 1935 season, the Crawfords faced the New York Cubans in the playoff for the Negro National League championship. The Cubans led by 3 games to 2. Game 6 was tied when Johnson came up to bat with the bases loaded in the ninth. The count stood at 3 and 2 when he smacked a grass-cutter down the right field line. The New York first baseman juggled the ball and the Crawfords had tied the series. They won the next game 8 to 7 for the title.

Following the season the Crawfords were barnstorming near Shreveport, Louisiana. They were traveling in two cars over dirt roads, when Judy and the other occupants of his car came upon the Crawfords' second car overturned in a ditch. The vehicle had flipped over three times, breaking the car's canvas top, but the nine players had jumped out and were not hurt. "That was a miracle," remembered Judy, "And when Oscar Charleston got out he had a piece of the steering wheel—they were wood then—in each of his hands. He was powerful."

In 1936, after the Crawfords again won the pennant, Johnson retired. For a time, he coached the Alco Flashes, a semipro basketball team that became the Delaware State Champions in 1937. Judy was a driver for the Continental Cab Company in Wilmington until 1954, when the Philadelphia Athletics hired him to sniff out talent during the club's final season in Philadelphia. Later, Johnson drove a school bus, and he and his brother John opened a general store in the Hillside community.

While Judy worked in Wilmington, he watched as white major league players entered the Hall of Fame. He and countless other Negro Leagues players were not even considered for baseball's highest honor until 1971, when Satchel Paige became the first of their ranks to be inducted. Since then, the Committee on Negro Baseball Leagues has selected one Negro Leagues player annually for induction.

Judy Johnson accepts a plaque from baseball commissioner Bowie Kuhn at Hall of Fame in-duction ceremonies in 1975.

Judy hoped he might be chosen during his lifetime, but as each year passed he grew more doubtful. When questioned about the subject he replied, "You have to take the bitter with the sweet."

Finally, on February 10, 1975, Judy received the news that he would be the sixth Negro Leagues player to be inducted into the Hall of Fame. The seventy-four-year-old Johnson was elated. "This is the happiest day in my life except when I married my wife," he told reporters. "I'm glad I got it while I'm still living. That was my wish."

However, in March, Judy suffered a heart attack. His family and friends feared he would be unable to attend the induction ceremonies in Cooperstown, New York, that summer. But despite his age and his health problems, Johnson's determination was strong. On August 18, 1975, he accepted his plaque from Commissioner Bowie Kuhn before a crowd of 7,500.

Although other players were inducted that day, Judy's words produced the most emotional response at the ceremonies. "Everyone's been so good to me. I had good times and bad times in my baseball career, but I enjoyed most of them," he told the audience as he held his hands to his face and wept. The crowd rose to give him a standing ovation. Resuming his speech, he said, "It'll never get out of me. I guess I'll die with a baseball in my hand. I just love the game."

Judy Johnson died on June 15, 1989, at the Tilton Terrace health care facility. A religious man, Johnson and his wife belonged to the Haven United Methodist Church where, at the time of his death, he had been a member longer than anyone else. He is buried in the Silverbrook Cemetery on Lancaster and DuPont Roads in Wilmington. A playing field in Wilmington is named for him.

5

If they said, "Come on, here's a steak dinner," and I had a chance to go out and play a game of baseball, I'd go out and play the game and let the steak sit there.
— Lefty Grove

Robert Moses "Lefty "Grove

Robert Moses Grove was born on March 6, 1900, in Lonaconing, Maryland, a mining community located in the state's western panhandle in the Allegheny Mountains. "Coney," as residents called it, was home to three coal mines, a silk mill, and a glass factory. The boomtown was dominated by a coal mining company whose superintendent had the power to fire workers who displeased him for any reason. While the miners lived in cramped dwellings that hugged the hillsides, the superintendent lived in a stately white house that towered above Coney's narrow streets.

Many of Coney's residents worked in the mines, trying to eke out a modest living. Money was deducted from the miners' salaries to pay for doctor bills, school fees, and purchases from the community store. Fifty cents a month insured a family's medical expenses. Mining families tried to raise much of their own food by growing a vegetable garden and by keeping a cow and some chickens.

John Grove, Robert's father, earned fifty cents a ton for the soft coal he picked from the Waynesburg Mine in Midland, and his three eldest sons joined him in that labor.

Like other miners, the Grove men entered the mines before sunup, crouching in the small wagons that carried them into the underground shafts. They often toiled past sundown, crawling through the low tunnels where they worked on their knees.

Robert, the seventh child of John and Emma Beeman Grove, attended the Charlestown School, a two-room school for grades one through eight. The Grove children grew up under the watchful eye of their mother, a petite woman with delicate features, who declared that although she had to look up to her sons, she was the boss.

When not in school, the boys played baseball with any equipment they could produce: a fencepost made a fine bat, while a stone wrapped with cloth and tape would be the ball. A real baseball cost twenty-five cents and the Grove family, like many others in the coal-mining region, could not spare "two bits."

"We made our own," Grove recalled. "We'd get some old wool socks, unravel them and, using a cork stopper for a center, wind ourselves a ball." Occasionally one of the boys received a twenty-five-cent Rocket, but in no time the cover would tear away and the sphere would be carefully mended with layers of thick black tape. If one of the baseballs landed in the Groves' vegetable garden, Robert's father would retrieve it and keep it in the house for a while to discourage the boys from playing near the house. Robert lobbed countless stones over a railroad track nestled high on a hill at the end of his street.

In the early 1900s, Walter Johnson was the Washington Senators star pitcher. The nation's capital was a train ride away from Lonaconing. When they had train fare and the price of admission to a Senators game, Lonaconing residents went to see the ace hurler they called the Big Train. Grove remembered seeing "that bugger pitch . . . Down around the knees—whoosh! One after another. I pitched against a lot of guys and saw a lot of guys throw and I haven't seen one yet close to as fast as he was."

An education held little value in the coal-mining region at that time. Like thousands of others, Robert dropped out of school after the eighth grade so that he could contribute to his large family's income. When he substituted for one of his brothers in the mines, he immediately disliked the work. After two weeks he quit, telling his father, "Dad, I didn't put the coal in there and and I hope I don't have to take no more of her out."

When the United States entered World War I in 1917, industries spread to small communities such as Lonaconing, bringing new jobs. Robert drove spikes for the railroad crews and he worked in the glass factory, where flames belched from huge furnaces. Then he moved to the silk mill as a bobbin boy, tending the gigantic spinning spools of silk thread. The entire town kept time by the mill's shrill whistle as it sounded morning and night. Eventually, Robert became a mechanic's assistant in one of the railroad shops in nearby Cumberland. The trains were parked in brick roundhouses, where their huge steam engines were disassembled and the cylinders cleaned.

In contrast to the dreary surroundings of the factories and mines, baseball offered sunshine and fresh air. The local team, Midland, charged twenty-five cents admission to the Saturday afternoon games, and the players divided the receipts. After church and dinner on Sundays, the men and boys of the town gathered at First Field, a level stretch of ground hidden by trees in back of the Big Vein Mine.

With Midland as his only baseball experience, in 1920 the twenty-year-old Grove won a tryout with the Martinsburg, West Virginia, club in the Blue Ridge League. Years later Grove was asked if it was true that he rode a bicycle to the tryout. "Who ever heard of riding a bike in the mountains?" he snapped. "I walked!"

He landed a spot as a first baseman, but soon manager Bill Louden put the fiery southpaw on the mound, where Robert logged 60 strikeouts in 59 innings. A frustrated pitcher from the rival Hagerstown club, worried that Grove spelled doom for his team that season, may have tipped off Walter Fewster, a trainer for the International League Baltimore Orioles. Fewster relayed the news of Grove's blazing fastball to the club's owner, Jack Dunn.

Martinsburg, a new franchise with little money, had managed to acquire a playing field and erect a modest grandstand, but the team could not afford to build an outfield fence. Jack Dunn offered Martinsburg $3,100 for their lanky, young pitcher. "For that money you can build a fence all the way around the park," he said. It was an offer they couldn't refuse. Soon, Robert Moses Grove was on a train to Baltimore.

Grove's background in Lonaconing hadn't prepared him for life on a city team. Shy and quiet, he was not used to the harsh treatment given rookies. Grove remembered, "It was rough on a kid trying to make it in baseball in those days. I was with the Baltimore Orioles two weeks before anybody spoke to me."

While Grove found the Orioles unfriendly, others remembered him as a private young man whose temper ignited if things didn't go well on the field. But no one disputed his talent on the mound; the southpaw could "bring it." A sportswriter attributed Lefty's talents to his pioneer ancestry, describing, "the kind of folks who used to be able to shoot the seeds out of apples with their squirrel rifles. He can shoot almost that well himself . . . some of the American League batters insist he shoots baseballs at them out of a hidden rifle."

Grove remained with the Orioles for the next four seasons, striking out more than 1,100 batters with 109 wins and 36 losses. Baltimore, in the midst of a seven-year pennant-winning streak, was under no pressure to unload their talented stars.

While in Baltimore, Lefty married Ethel Matthews but the couple made their home in Lonaconing during the off-season. The Groves eventually had two children, Robert Jr. and Doris.

In 1924, Connie Mack, the owner-manager of the Philadelphia A's, paid $100,600 for Grove's contract, the most money ever paid for a player up to that time. Because Lefty's name had appeared in the Orioles box scores as "Groves," Mr. Mack referred to his ace southpaw as Groves to the press. But when he addressed Lefty directly, Mr. Mack always called him Robert.

Two future Hall of Fame players made their major league debuts on April 14, 1925. The twenty-five-year-old Robert Moses Grove took the mound before 22,000 fans on opening day at Shibe Park, and rookie catcher Mickey Cochrane pinch-hit in the eighth inning. For the next eight years the pair formed an incredible battery, helping the A's capture three pennants and two World Series.

However, the rookie southpaw got off to a shaky start in his first major league game. He walked four and hit a batter before Connie Mack pulled him in the fourth inning. By the end of the season, he led the league in strikeouts with 116. As wild as he was fast, he also led in walks with 131.

Like his childhood hero Walter Johnson, Grove threw nothing but fastballs, prompting sportswriter Bugs Baer to declare, "Grove could throw a lamb chop past a wolf." Another writer described Grove's

Lefty Grove stands in the outfield in Oriole Park in the 1920s. On the scoreboard behind him, scores were posted by placing numbers in the openings by hand.

three pitches as "fast, faster, and fastest." Hall of Fame shortstop Joe Sewell, who rarely struck out, said, "Sometimes when the sun was out, really bright, he would throw that baseball in there and it looked like a flash of white sewing thread coming up at you . . . Inning after inning, he never slowed up. He could stand out there for a week, and barrel it in at you."

Despite his amazing speed and toughness, Grove worked through some rough spots during his rookie year. A's catcher Mickey Cochrane remembered helping the young hurler. "Lefty suffered from a fault, common among good strong pitchers with little experience. He took his eyes off the plate during his windup—an error that frequently happens when young pitchers are concentrating on their windup."

Lefty won 10 and and lost 12 in 1925 and was 13-13 the following season. In 1927 he began seven consecutive 20-win seasons.

The A's dynasty reigned with the incredible pitching staff of Grove, Ed Rommel, Rube Walberg, and George Earnshaw. Behind them were Philadelphia's sluggers: Jimmie Foxx, Al Simmons, and Cochrane. In 1929 they snapped the Yankees' string of three straight American League pennants. Grove won the first of four consecutive ERA titles.

Manager Mack not only relied on his starters to go the distance, he also used them in relief. When the A's met the Chicago Cubs in the 1929 World Series, Connie Mack used Grove only in relief. Lefty threw smoke in six shutout innings as Philadelphia grabbed the crown in five contests.

In 1930 Grove led the American League with 28 wins. In the World Series against the St. Louis Cardinals he and George Earnshaw pitched 44 of the 52 innings, splitting four wins. Grove's Maryland teammate Jimmie Foxx helped him win Game 5 by hitting a two-run homer in the ninth.

During spring training in 1931, coach Kid Gleason thought Grove's control would improve if Lefty didn't work so fast. He suggested Lefty

Lefty poses with some young Philadelphia fans around 1930. In those days starting pitchers were expected to go nine innings and relieve too. In 1931 and 1932, Grove completed 54 of his 60 starts and relieved in 31 other games.

try counting to ten between pitches. "The doctor's orders were soon grapevined around the league," recalled Mickey Cochrane. "All the bench jockeys on the circuit were quickly counting ten on every pitch Lefty made. But it never bothered his control, and they stopped it after a while."

Lefty was just wild enough and ornery enough to keep hitters jittery at the plate. "Never bothered me who was up there with the bat. I'd hit 'em in the middle of the back or hit 'em in the foot, it didn't make any difference to me. But I'd never throw at a man's head. Never believed in it."

In contrast to his on-the-field intensity, Grove was a quiet, disciplined man off the diamond who kept himself in good condition year round. During the season Lefty ended each day with an after-dinner cigar, his single daily smoke. He was friendly, but preferred to keep to himself, and was known as a loner. By eight o'clock in the evening he was in his room, where he read a wild west magazine until turning off the lights at nine. In the winter the western Maryland pitching ace returned to Lonaconing, where no one talked to him about baseball.

Despite his quiet nature, Lefty's reputation for throwing temper tantrums soon equaled his fame for fanning batters. In 1931 Grove had won 16 straight games to tie a 1912 record set by the Red Sox Smokey Joe Wood and the Senators Walter Johnson. Going after his 17th victory in St. Louis against the Browns, two men were out and one on in the third when rookie left fielder Jim Moore misjudged a fly ball. It dropped behind him, a run scored, and Philadelphia lost 1 to 0. Moore had been substituting that day for Philadelphia's star outfielder, Al Simmons, who'd taken the day off to see a doctor.

Immediately following the last out, Grove stormed to the clubhouse, cursing Simmons who, of course, was not present. A's outfielder Doc Cramer remembered, "The sparks were flying off Grove.

Oh I mean to tell you. I knew it was going to happen. Well, he was about three lockers down from me. I saw him stand up and take hold of the top of his shirt with both hands—we had buttons on our shirts in those days—stand like that for a second, and then rip! He tore that shirt apart so fast and so hard that I saw the buttons go flying past me, three lockers away.

"Then everything went flying—bats, balls, gloves, shoes, benches. He broke up a couple of lockers. Nobody said a word. There was no point. You had to wait till the steam went out of him. Next day he was all right. But I never will forget those buttons flying past me."

Moore remained in the dugout during Lefty's tirade, wisely waiting for the pitcher to calm down. Lefty later excused his tantrum by explaining, "I didn't say anything to Jim Moore, 'cause he was just a young guy just come to the team and he never played in St. Louis. It was Simmons' fault. He's the one I blame for it." Although he went on to win six more consecutive contests, Lefty's chance to claim 23 straight wins had died in left field. The disappointment never left him.

Sometimes Jimmy Dykes could help Lefty calm down during a game. "I was his good friend off the field, so I was the only one allowed to go near him on the mound," explained Dykes. " If his blood pressure was going up, I would get the ball and hold it for a while."

When asked about his temper, Lefty spoke openly. "Did I get sore at my teammates? Did I yell at Joe Cronin (the Red Sox manager)? Yes sir. Yes I did," explained Grove. "I was out there to win. That's the only way to play the game."

Years later Grove watched a frustrated rookie pitcher injure his foot when he kicked a water bucket following a loss. Speaking from experience, Lefty advised the young player, "Kid, when you kick a water bucket never kick it with your toes. Always use the side of your foot."

Grove led the American League in strikeouts each of his first seven seasons, inspiring a base-ball writer to declare, "Grove could throw a lamb chop past a wolf."

Grove won 31 games and lost 5 in 1931 as the A's captured the American League pennant and faced the Cardinals in the World Series. Once more, Grove and Earnshaw teamed up, this time pitching 50 of the 61 innings in seven games, but the Cards defeated the A's.

In 1933 the Yankees had gone 308 games without being shut out when Lefty faced them. Firing heat all afternoon, Grove ended that phenomenal streak, blanking the New Yorkers 7 to 0. He fanned six, getting Ruth to whiff three times and Gehrig twice.

In another game, Connie Mack brought in his ace left-hander in relief against the Yankees with the bases loaded and none out. He threw only ten pitches, and fanned the Babe, Lou Gehrig, and Tony Lazzeri to end the inning. Babe compared Grove and Walter Johnson. "They were sweet to hit. They were just cousins. Walter Johnson and Grove were just as fast as a rifle shot."

Despite the success of Mack's troops, Philadelphia increasingly felt the effects of the depression. Not only did A's fans have less money for baseball tickets, they seemed bored by their team's success. Falling attendance forced Connie Mack to unload his best players. Although Grove led the league with 24 wins, he was sold to the Red Sox at the end of the 1933 season.

Lefty's career in Boston began on a down note. A sore arm plagued him throughout 1934, but he rebounded the following year to win 20 games, the final such season of his career.

Grove's solid 1935 season started poorly. When he reported for spring training in Florida he felt ill, and even considered quitting baseball. The doctors found that he was suffering from several infected teeth. Grove missed spring training; when Lefty finally took the mound that season, his fingers lacked the tough skin pitchers usually developed in the spring. One day in Detroit he had just struck out a batter in the fifth inning when his catcher threw the ball to third baseman Bill Werber, who noticed blood on the ball. Instead of throwing it to the shortstop, Werber took the ball to the mound. Showing the ball to Lefty he said, "There's blood all over the ball. What's the matter with you?"

Werber noticed there was no skin on Grove's pitching fingers. "Lefty, you can't pitch like that."

"You play third base and I'll do the pitching," Grove snapped.

At thirty-five, Grove was still driven by the fire-in-the-belly competitiveness he'd always possessed. Bill Werber explained the veteran pitcher's toughness. "Lefty didn't want to be beaten—ever. He wasn't one of these guys who throw 60, 70, 80, 90, or 100 pitches and look to the dugout as if to say, 'I've thrown my hundred pitches and it's time for me to come out.' If the game went 13, 14, or 15 innings without a decision, he didn't want the manager to come out of that dugout."

Grove won his 300th game on July 25, 1941, against the Cleveland Indians. He finished at 7-7 that season, and joked, "I'm throwing the ball as fast as ever. It's just not getting there as fast." Following the season, Boston handed him his unconditional release. At forty-one, his career had ended. "The old boy just played out after 21 years, 17 in the big leagues," said Grove, referring to his pitching arm.

During his career, Lefty had traveled to Japan with an All-Star team of major leaguers. As a token of friendship, the Japanese had presented the southpaw with a giant glove with both the American and the Japanese flags painted on it. When the Japanese bombed Pearl Harbor on December 7, 1941, Lefty used a knife to scrape away the Japanese flag, leaving the stars and stripes intact.

Without the pressure of the big leagues, Lefty retired in Lonaconing and mellowed into a man who enjoyed smoking a pipe and talking with townsfolk over breakfast each morning at Marshall's cafe. He owned a bowling alley and settled into the pace of small town life. He was inducted into the Baseball Hall of Fame in 1947.

A trio of 1925 rookies from the Philadelphia A's get together with Kansas City A's manager Lou Boudreau in the mid-1950s. From left to right, *Mickey Cochrane, Jimmie Foxx, Lefty Grove, and Boudreau.*

The Philadelphia A's

Led by future Hall of Famers Al Simmons, Mickey Cochrane, Lefty Grove, and Jimmie Foxx, the Philadelphia A's ruled the American League from 1929 through 1931. Their manager, Connie Mack, started the team in the new American League in 1901 and managed the A's for fifty years. The team moved to Kansas City in 1955, and to Oakland in 1968.

Eventually Grove moved to Norwalk, Ohio, where his son Robert Jr. had made his home. He died there on May 22, 1975. His obituary in the *New York Times* described him as "a tall, genial gentleman of 75 with a head of lustrous white hair who loved to sit around at baseball gatherings cutting up old touches [reminiscing]."

In describing his love for baseball, Lefty said, "If they said, 'Come on, here's a steak dinner,' and I had a chance to go out and play a game of baseball, I'd go out and play the game and let the steak sit there. I would."

6

Let me get a good grip on the bat, as if I wanted to leave my fingerprints on the wood: let me swing with a snap which comes from a powerful wrist, and when I've gotten back of the ball, it sure will travel.

—Jimmie Foxx

James Emory "Double X" Foxx

The Cubs had just won the 1907 World Series by sweeping the Tigers in four games with one tie when James Emory Foxx was born on October 22 near Sudlersville, a small town in Queen Anne's County on Maryland's Eastern Shore. The baby's parents, Samuel Dell Foxx and Mattie Smith Foxx, were tenant farmers. Having just completed the season's harvest, they welcomed the birth of their first child, Jim. In those days, farmers had no electricity and no mechanized equipment such as tractors; a son meant an extra pair of hands to help with the work.

There was another reason the elder Foxx, known as Mr. Dell, was delighted to have a boy; he loved baseball. Since dairy cows required milking twice daily, leisure travel for farmers was impossible, but a weekly game of baseball provided a welcome respite from the eternal chores. Mr. Foxx, catcher for the town team, hoped that his son would grow to share his enthusiasm for the game. As soon as Jim was able to sit up, his father rolled a ball across the floor to him. Jim's cousin Mildred Barracliff remembered, "By the time he was eight, he was catching the ball as hard as his father could throw it."

Dominated by strict Methodists, the local populace observed religious dictates that did not allow work or sports activity on Sunday. Baseball games played on Saturday were eagerly anticipated throughout the week. After the afternoon game and the evening milking, the residents of Sudlersville donned their best clothes for an evening stroll downtown, a custom of the pre-automobile era. The region's southern culture was reflected in the manners the Foxxes taught their children, requiring them to respect their elders and to behave in a humble way, refraining from loud, bold actions.

Like many farm boys, Jim and his younger brother, Samuel Dell, helped their parents on the farm. The daily routine seldom varied. The entire family woke up at 4:30 A.M. After the morning milking, the boys carried the brimming buckets of warm milk from the barn to the milkhouse and emptied them into large metal cans. The heavy cans were hoisted onto a horse-drawn wagon for the trip to the town cooling station, where the milk was chilled before being transported by train to dairies in the city. The boys then walked a mile to the local elementary school at Benton's Corners.

When Jimmie Foxx was growing up, almost every Maryland town had a team that played other towns. At thirteen, Foxx, first row, right, *caught for the Sudlersville team.*

Town Team Ball

When we say that baseball's popularity grew immensely in the United States between 1880 and 1950, we usually think of professional baseball. . . . Yet another level of baseball has been ignored. It was that level of baseball that was then closest to most Americans. . . . Almost every small town and city neighborhood, as well as mills and even churches, had organized amateur and/or semi-professional baseball teams in these years, before they began to disappear in the 1950s. (From an article by Frank Keetz in *The National Pastime: A Review of Baseball History*)

Later, when Jim went to Sudlersville High School, he would drive the wagon to the station before school, hitch up the horses, and return after school to take them home.

When crops failed, the milk check provided a farmer's only earnings. Even during good years, tenant farmers usually didn't have "two nickels to rub together on Saturday night." As Jim and Sammy Dell grew up, the Foxxes were rarely able to scrape together the ten cents their sons needed to see a movie in nearby Chestertown.

It took strong arms to lift heavy bales of hay or bags of fertilizer, to swing an ax, guide a team of horses, or haul buckets of water from an outside pump. Jim thrived on the steady diet of hard work and country food. By 1920 he was a muscular 5-foot, 11-inch thirteen-year-old weighing 185 pounds. Built like a sturdy oak, his arms rippled with muscles and his thick brown hair crowned a handsome face that often sported a wide grin.

Despite his youth, Jim played baseball on the town team with the older boys and men. At fifteen, he earned his first money playing baseball when a team in a nearby county paid him five dollars a game to catch for them. It was the most money the teenager's brawny hand had ever held.

Jim's teammates never forgot his performance as a catcher for the school team. First baseman Ed Walraven recalled, "I had a two-dollar mitt. Foxx threw so hard my hand was hurting from the first day. It took me until past soccer season before it healed." Bernard Merrick, who played second, described Foxx's strength. "Jim could squat down behind home plate and throw to second on a line drive without getting up. The pitcher had to duck to save his life."

Jim also excelled in basketball and soccer, but his favorite sport was track. He idolized Charlie Paddock, the 1920 Olympic champion sprinter, and dreamed of becoming a great runner. In 1923 the Baltimore sportswriters named him Maryland's outstanding athlete. He held eight track titles, including the broad jump, the high jump, and sprints from 50 to 440 yards. Allowed to enter only two events at the state Olympiad, he chose the high jump and the 220-yard dash, easily taking both events.

That same year, a county all-star baseball team formed to play teams outside Maryland. Jim not only caught for the team, he proved his versatility by playing third base and the outfield. His talents at the plate were as good as his defensive skills. He ended the season batting .454 and followed that performance by hitting .552 for Sudlersville High in 1924.

One evening that spring, Dell Foxx and Jimmie visited Frank "Home Run" Baker, the former star of the Philadelphia A's and New York Yankees who lived in Trappe in nearby Talbot County. Baker was the manager of the Easton club in the Eastern Shore League. Dell Foxx asked Baker, "Will you give my boy a chance with your ball club?"

"A quick glance at the big, 16-year-old youngster told me all I had to know," recalled Baker. "If this kid can play baseball, I thought, he's got to be good. I told Mr. Foxx to have Jimmie at Federal Park in Easton the next day."

Jim worked out with the Easton club, then went back to the farm and thought no more about it. A few days later, a penny postcard arrived inviting him to join the Easton Farmers. At first Jim thought it was a joke. "I thought somebody was trying to needle me," he later recalled. "Maybe a couple of the cut-ups that hung around the general store in Sudlersville sent it. But when I saw the postmark was Trappe, I decided nobody would go to that much trouble to play a prank."

Jim, now a 6-foot, 195-pounder, signed for $100 a month for four months, more than he'd ever dreamed he would earn. He saw it as a great summer job preceding his senior year of high school.

On May 31 it seemed as if the entire town of Sudlersville was on hand to watch Jim play his first game in Easton. They were rewarded when he hit a home run out of Federal Park during the local team's losing effort. As Baker watched the ball soar over the fence, he was convinced that Foxx was big league material.

Several stories exist about how Foxx went to the major leagues. What is clear is that Baker told both of his former big league teams, the Yankees and the Philadelphia A's, about the talented farmboy. Bill Werber, Foxx's teammate with the Boston Red Sox, often went hunting with Home Run Baker. According to Werber, Baker told him of taking Foxx to New York, where manager Miller Huggins had a first glimpse of the young catcher. "He can knock the cover off the ball, play any position, run like a deer, and throw golf balls," Baker told the Yankee skipper. Huggins told him they couldn't use the youngster.

Baker then went to Philadelphia and visited Connie Mack, who listened to his former star and replied, "Bake, if he's as good as you say, I'll take him and I don't even want to see him first." The A's bought Foxx's contract for $2,500.

On September 10, Foxx had just played his last game of the season when he was called to the telephone. It was Connie Mack inviting him to join the A's on a western road trip the next day. Foxx made his only appearance with the A's that season during an exhibition game in Erie, Pennsylvania, hitting a game-winning triple.

By his seventeenth birthday on October 22, Foxx was back on the farm and in classes at Sudlersville High. However, in February 1925, an envelope arrived from the A's with a contract for $2,000 and a letter inviting him to spring training. Despite his mother's pleas that he graduate from school first, Jim's hope of a career in the majors won out.

On Friday, February 20, Foxx boarded a Florida-bound train in Baltimore with pitchers Art Stokes, Eddie Rommel, and a rookie named Lefty Grove. On the train they met rookie catcher Mickey Cochrane. Grove and Cochrane were the A's most promising prospects. The A's had paid $106,000 for Grove, the strikeout king of the International League. Cochrane, a .350 hitter in the minors, cost the A's $50,000.

At first Foxx seemed eclipsed by his fellow rookies, but Connie Mack recognized the boy's potential. As reporters praised Cochrane one day, the A's manager replied, "Yes, I think I landed a great player in Cochrane. But standing over there is the boy that attracts my eye."

Squinting beyond Mack's pointed finger, they listened to the respected manager's predictions. "There he is. That big youngster warming up the pitchers. His name is Jimmie Foxx," he explained. "He's the dandy of them all. He's going to be the greatest player in the land some day. He may not look so much to you fellows now. He's green and lacks experience, and he doesn't know how to handle himself. But if I ever saw a diamond in the rough, it's that lad. And he is fast. He looks like a little truck, but he gets over the ground."

Mack, a brilliant manager, also realized that Foxx required seasoning before he could become a successful big leaguer. He had seen the careers of many youngsters ruined by being pushed too rapidly. He wanted his diamond in the rough to first watch and learn. When the 1925 season opened, Foxx watched the A's catcher, Mickey Cochrane, from the bench. Later, Foxx played for the A's minor league club in Providence, Rhode Island, where he benefited from playing daily.

Foxx saw little action in 1926, appearing in only 26 games and hitting .313. The A's used Foxx at first base in 1927 when he appeared in 61 games. The season provided one of his greatest thrills: his first home run. He would go on to hit 534 roundtrippers, but he treasured his first, later telling reporters, "I remember more about the first homer I ever hit, because I was just a boy, and it meant something to me."

Connie Mack realized the A's needed Foxx's clout at the plate, but he had to find a place for him in the field. Mickey Cochrane was the best catcher in baseball. Jimmie had to find another position.

In 1928 the A's alternated Foxx between first and third. (Before his career ended in 1945, he had played every position except second base.) While his defensive skills were strong, he exploded at the plate, finishing the season hitting .328 with 13 home runs. The A's finished only 3 games behind New York, which captured the American League pennant for the third consecutive season. Foxx capped off the year by eloping with Helen Hite the day after Christmas.

When the 1929 season opened, Foxx became Philadelphia's first baseman. By June 1, Foxx's average soared to over .400. Vendors under the grandstand could tell when Foxx connected for a home run, just by the unique sound of it. When October arrived the A's had easily clinched the American League pennant, outdistancing the Yankees by 16 games. They faced the Chicago Cubs in the World Series, which opened in Chicago on October 8. The first game was deadlocked until the seventh inning, when Foxx blasted a home run, spurring the A's 3-1 win. The next day he slammed a three-run homer as Philadelphia trounced the Cubs 9 to 3. The Series then moved to Shibe Park and the Cubs took the third game 3 to 1.

In Game 4 on October 12, the Cubs were leading Philadelphia 8 to 0 as the A's came up to bat in the last of the seventh. The A's then staged the most incredible comeback in Series history. They had scored seven runs and trailed 8 to 7 when Foxx stepped to the plate for the second time in the inning, with Cochrane on second and Simmons on first. He felt the beads of sweat on his neck and hands as he stared out at the pitcher, Sheriff Blake, who Foxx recalled "seemed to be a little man standing far off at the small end of a telescope."

"'Well Foxx,' I said to myself. 'Get in there. You either do or you don't.' I took a deep breath and swung at one of Blake's slants and drove a single to center. Mickey was off like a demon, rounding third and tearing for home before I reached first base. (Jimmy) Dykes then drove in two more runs with a double. When I reached the bench,

Connie Mack looked at me and said, 'Nice work, boy. You got the big hit.'" The A's won 10 to 8.

Philadelphia won the World Series the next day with a ninth-inning rally. October marked many milestones in Foxx's life. His first child, James Emory Foxx Jr., was born on October 3; he had hit three home runs with men on base in his first World Series; and he had received $5,620.57 as his share of the players' pool. He celebrated his twenty-second birthday on October 22, and he invested all his championship earnings in Wall Street's soaring stock market. The future had never looked better. But on October 29, the stock market crashed and Foxx lost every cent he'd invested.

Philadelphia won the World Series again in 1930, defeating the St. Louis Cardinals in 6 games. As the country plunged into the Great Depression, Foxx felt fortunate to sign a three-year contract with the A's for $50,000. In 1931 Philadelphia won their third straight pennant and again faced the Cardinals, but St. Louis turned the tables on the reigning world champs, grabbing the Series 4 to 3. Although Foxx hit 30 homers that season, his average fell to .291.

In 1932 Foxx was hitting .457 by the end of April. He had fulfilled all of Connie Mack's predictions. Every American league pitcher feared facing Jim. Despite a sprained wrist, he finished the season batting .364 with a league-leading 169 RBI. He also slammed 58 home runs, the record for right-handed hitters. His feats earned him the American League Most Valuable Player award. He repeated as MVP in 1933, winning the triple crown (leading in batting average, home runs, and RBI).

Foxx commanded respect each time he stepped into the batter's box. White Sox pitcher Ted Lyons said that Foxx's biceps "seemed to carry 35 pounds-per-square-inch of air in them." The Yankees jovial southpaw Lefty Gomez joked, "I tried wearing glasses to improve my pitching. The first time I wore them and looked at Foxx, it scared me

Lou Gehrig and Foxx were teammates in the first All-Star game in 1933. Gehrig hit 493 homers in his fourteen year career. Foxx hit 534 during his sixteen years in the majors.

to death. His arms looked like telephone poles, and every time he squeezed the bat I could see sawdust drip. I threw away my glasses."

Fans and players alike remembered Foxx's home runs. He hit the ball harder and farther than anybody else during his twenty-year career. He hit four over the left field roof at Comiskey Park. One Shibe Park shot measured 500 feet. At Yankee Stadium he hit one of Lefty Gomez's pitches into the upper left field stands, smashing a seat into splinters. Whenever he connected, the sound of bat mashing ball left no doubt as to who had hit it.

Bill Werber, who weighed 170 pounds, remembered his teammate's strength from a personal demonstration. "One day I made myself stiff and Foxx picked me up by the ankles, lifting me as high as his chest."

Foxx's sturdy forearms and formidable biceps made him appear fierce, but he was equally known for his easygoing nature. "Foxxie is the easiest boy on the team to handle," declared Connie Mack. "He does whatever I ask him to do with never a word of complaint." While some players showed hot tempers and massive egos, the A's slugger, whom the sportswriters dubbed "Double X" and "the Beast," was as cool as a glass of iced tea. Rather than joining on-the-field confrontations, Foxx squatted on his haunches at first base and waited for the storm to blow over.

When major league baseball's first All-Star Game took place in 1933 in Chicago, the fans elected Foxx to the American League team. He appeared in seven All-Star contests before his retirement.

At age twenty-six, Foxx's star was blazing brightly, but the Great Depression had dimmed his economic worth. Many Americans could no longer afford even the small luxury of a baseball ticket, and the A's attendance plummeted. To cut their payroll the team sold most of their top stars. Despite Foxx's brilliant performances over the past two years, when his contract expired at the end of the 1933 season the A's offered him only $11,000, a 30 percent cut in salary. He finally settled for $18,000.

Foxx's bank account paled in comparison to that of Babe Ruth, the game's highest-paid player, but his taste for the good life and his generosity to others equaled the Great Bambino's. Like Ruth, Double X enjoyed life, buying fancy cars, wearing stylish clothes, and savoring the nightlife. The former farmboy often picked up his teammates' tabs, and lavishly tipped restaurant and hotel employees.

Billy Sullivan, a former White Sox player, remembered Foxx's generosity during Sullivan's rookie year. The young first baseman from Notre Dame had just finished infield practice one day. Foxx was walking onto the field as the rookie left his post. "When I was finished I threw my glove on the ground, the way we did in those days. Foxx picked it up," he recalled. "As I was walking away, he called me over. 'We don't use gloves like this up here,' he said. 'It's too small.'

"I told him it was the only one I could find in South Bend. The next day he came out with two gloves. He handed me one that was all broken in just right and said, 'Take it, it's yours.'"

Foxx was generous to his family back in Sudlersville too. He bought his parents a farm, but unfortunately Dell and Mattie lost their land to bank foreclosure during the depression. When Sammy Dell needed cash, his big brother always came through.

In 1934 Philadelphia slid to fifth place. Double X continued to put up the numbers, batting .334 with 130 RBI and 44 home runs, but Philadelphia's descent worsened. In 1935 the A's fell to last place despite Foxx's league-leading 36 home runs and his .346 batting average. Once again he made the All-Star team, driving in three runs in the American League's 4-1 victory.

Foxx began 1936 with a new team and a new son, William Kenneth, who arrived in May. The A's had sold Jim to the Boston Red Sox, and delighted Boston fans turned out to see the Beast wearing a Red Sox

*After being named the American League's Most Valuable Player in 1932
and 1933 with the Philadelphia A's, Foxx moved to Boston in 1936 and
won his third MVP for the Red Sox in 1938.*

uniform. Almost sixty years later long-time fan Bill Mullen described the first time he saw Foxx. "I was taken to my first major league game at Fenway Park in 1936, and I have no sharp recollections of opponent or score," he said. "But I do remember looking in awe at Mr. Foxx and his bulging biceps. To a scrawny 9-year-old, he was larger than life yet ever so seemingly joyful in his time, place, and abilities. From that day on, I devoured the Red Sox box scores, feasting on his performances." Foxx ended the season hitting .338 with 41 homers.

In October Foxx returned to the Eastern Shore to appear in two local baseball games in Cambridge, where teams sponsored by Coca-Cola and the Phillips Packing Company were great rivals. (Phillips produced canned goods, such as Phillips Delicious Tomatoes.) At the end of the season the two teams met for the city championship in a best-of-seven series played in weekly Sunday games at the Fairgrounds Park.

The teams split the first four games, then gradually brought in professional players to bolster their lineups. On October 4 the clubs met for Game 5 with 3,000 fans looking on as Jimmie Foxx and a few of his Boston teammates came out wearing Phillips uniforms. Foxx drove one more than 400 feet over the center field fence; Phillips won 8 to 2, and led the series 3 to 2.

By the following week, Foxx had assembled more pros for Phillips; the team now featured nine big leaguers. Once again, they met Coca-Cola, and as 4,000 fans jammed the park, Phillips shut out their rival 2 to 0 to win the city championship.

Foxx's average fell to .296 in 1937 with 127 RBI and 36 home runs, but the following year he rebounded, winning his third Most Valuable Player trophy by launching 50 roundtrippers, and leading the league with 175 RBI and a .349 batting average. Boston climbed from fifth to second place behind Foxx's bat. Earlier that season, the St. Louis Browns had walked him six consecutive times, a remarkable display of respect for Double X's clout. At the end of the year, the Red Sox signed him for $27,000, sweetening the pot with $5,000 in bonuses, the most money he'd ever earned.

In 1939 a self-assured young player named Ted Williams joined Boston. Foxx and Williams seemed an unlikely duo. In contrast to Foxx's humble nature, Williams boasted about his prowess at the plate. Their physiques were polar opposites, but Williams's thin and lanky build belied his power at the plate. His biceps looked like Dell Foxx's lima bean poles compared to the veteran slugger's ample upper arms, but the teammates quickly became a double threat to American League pitchers.

An eleven-year-old Boston fan later remembered being visited by the two players while in the hospital. "One evening, long after the rigorously enforced visiting hours, a nurse said I had some special visitors—Mr. Foxx and a gangling, yet handsome young rookie, Theodore Samuel Williams. The nurses went slightly ga-ga over Teddy the Kid, but I just looked at Foxx like I was in the presence of the deity."

"I'll never forget my old teammate," Williams later said, "and how nicely he treated me as a young brash rookie, and what an impression he made on me when I first saw him. I don't believe anyone ever made the impact of the ball and bat sound like he did when he really got hold of it."

Describing his hitting motion, Foxx said, "Let me get a good grip on the bat, as if I wanted to leave my fingerprints on the wood; let me swing with a quick snap which comes from a powerful wrist; and when I've gotten back of the ball, it sure will travel."

By October Foxx had racked up 35 homers, averaging .360 at the plate. The 1939 season marked the zenith of Foxx's brilliant career. It also signaled the start of World War II as Hitler's troops invaded Poland on September 1, forever changing the world and ending a magnificent baseball era.

On August 16, 1940, Double X scalded two home runs over the fence against Washington. The first shot, his 30th of the season, made Foxx the only player to hit 30 or more home runs in twelve consecutive seasons. On his second homer he passed Lou Gehrig's career total of 493.

Foxx blasted his 500th home run on September 24 against the A's at Shibe Park, becoming the second player in the game's history to reach that number. He later downplayed the importance of that achievement, modestly comparing himself to a fellow Marylander. "After all," he said, "Babe Ruth hit 714."

After a slow start in 1942, Boston placed him on waivers and the Chicago Cubs picked him up on June 1. There he played with another slugging Eastern Shore farmboy, Bill "Swish" Nicholson. Foxx sat out the 1943 season, but the following year the Cubs asked him to return as a coach and occasional player. While with the Cubs he once again donned his catcher's gear when the team needed someone behind the plate during a game against the New York Giants. During his first at-bat he was nearly beaned when a ball emerged from the white shirts in the center field bleachers. Later, as he crouched behind the plate, a New York batter asked, "Jimmie, why don't you get out of here? You're going to get killed."

Foxx chuckled good-naturedly, "I got to eat, don't I?"

In fact, Double X's finances were no laughing matter. Foxx lost a lot of the money he'd invested in two golf courses when they were taken over by the government at the beginning of the war. Two of his business partners disappeared with $30,000. Jimmie Foxx was broke.

By 1945, many major league players were fighting in the war. Clubs filled their rosters with teens and aging veterans. Now thirty-seven and weighing 200 pounds, Foxx signed with the Philadelphia Blue Jays (now the Phillies) to play first and third. But when the club needed a pitcher in an exhibition game against the A's, Double X took the mound against his former team in Philadelphia. He pitched three scoreless innings before being relieved in the fourth. Later he started the second game of a doubleheader at home against the Reds. The veteran Foxx's fastball and screwball combined to give the Blue Jays a 4-1 lead going into the seventh before he was relieved. Heading for the showers, he received an ovation equaling any he'd received in his glory days. Philadelphia held on to win and Double X chalked up his only major league pitching victory.

The finest measure of Foxx's character and integrity was shown that day. His willingness to play whenever and wherever needed was as rare in baseball then as it is now. Almost a decade later, Boston sportswriter Buck O'Neil paid tribute to Double X, nominating him as the greatest of all ballplayers. "Ty Cobb was great and Ruth was mighty," he wrote, "but in team spirit Jimmie Foxx stands out above all others."

Embarking on a series of short-term jobs, Foxx managed the Fort Wayne Daisies of the All-American Girls Baseball League and he coached the University of Miami baseball team. He invested in a restaurant and worked as a salesman. He tried radio broadcasting and even driving a truck. His finances and his health worsened. "I had pride, but pride's not much good when you're flat broke," he told an interviewer. "I blew a lot of dough, and that's my fault. When you've been up and come down, a lot of people don't know you exist anymore. And a lot more think you've got a million dollars."

After suffering a heart attack, he could no longer work, but he received Social Security disability funds and some money from his twenty-year membership in the Association of Professional Ball Players. Foxx had retired just one year before the baseball players' pension began in 1946. "Baseball was mighty good to me," he said. "But I was born ten years too soon."

Foxx's notable career was capped when he was inducted into the Baseball Hall of Fame in the summer of 1951 along with Mel Ott.

Foxx was the strongest man in baseball. Often called "the Beast," he drove in a hundred or more runs in thirteen consecutive years. Here he holds a section of a telephone pole as a bat in a gag shot during spring training.

Double X's former skipper, Connie Mack, was there to honor the man he had signed on Home Run Baker's word twenty-seven years earlier.

With characteristic humility, Foxx addressed the Cooperstown audience. "All the years I played, all the great players I saw, played against, read about and watched, there always seemed to be so many great players. I never expected the honor. I'll never forget it."

During his retirement, Foxx lived in Florida. When his father died in Sudlersville, family members sent Jimmie cash so he could come home for his father's funeral. His last visit to Sudlersville occurred during the summer of 1966 when he and his brother Sammy Dell paid a call on their former high school teacher, Fannie B. Merrick. While Jimmie talked with Miss Fannie on the porch, his brother opened the trunk of their car to show a neighbor, Charles Palmatory, Jimmie's tarnished trophies. "No one cares about it anymore," he said.

Leaving Sudlersville, the two brothers stopped at Gil Dunn's pharmacy on nearby Kent Island. Double X had been Dunn's idol since his school days in Baltimore; now a pharmacist, he had created a Foxx Museum in his small store to honor his childhood hero. Hearing of Dunn's interest in him, Foxx stopped to give his things to the pharmacist. Jimmie strode into the store and introduced himself. "I was speechless," explained Dunn. "I know he could have sold those things, and I'm sure he needed the money, but he just gave them to me. He as much as told me I might as well have the things, as I seemed to care."

Jimmie Foxx left Dunn's pharmacy, crossed the Bay Bridge, and returned to Florida where he died a year later on July 21, 1967. He was fifty-nine years old.

On October 25, 1997, ninety years after Foxx's birth, the Sudlersville Betterment Club dedicated a life-size bronze statue of Jimmie Foxx, placing it at the intersection of roads Jimmie traveled countless times. Now all who pass through the town can pause to look upon the slugger as his bat slices a swath through eternity.

7

Desire is something you must have to make it in the majors.

—Al Kaline

Albert William "Al" Kaline

On October 7, 1968, Al Kaline stepped up to the plate with the bases loaded in the seventh inning of Game 5 of the World Series. The Detroit Tigers trailed the visiting St. Louis Cardinals 3 to 2. St. Louis led the Series 3 games to 1. If the Tigers lost Game 5, it would be all over. After sixteen years in the big leagues, this was Kaline's first World Series, and the hopes of every Detroit fan rode on his shoulders. It seemed that his entire career had come down to this single moment. Excited cheers filled the ballpark, the noise nearing explosive levels.

Detroit pitcher Mickey Lolich stood on third, thinking, "'There is Al Kaline, never played in a World Series.' I wanted him to get a base hit, for my sake naturally, and for the team's sake . . . If anybody could get that hit, I wanted it to be Al Kaline."

Cardinals left-hander Joe Hoerner fired his first pitch to Kaline, who fouled it off. The veteran slugger, a major leaguer since age eighteen, had long ago learned patience at the plate. As if teasing the lefty, he fouled off ball after ball waiting for the southpaw to deliver "his" pitch. Hoerner threw the next one high and Kaline pounced. With his arms fully extended, he scorched a crisp liner to right center. Mickey Lolich and Dick McAuliffe raced home. The Tigers took a 4-3 lead, and hung on to win 5 to 3. They took the next two games for their first World Series championship in twenty-three years. For Al, it was a childhood dream come true.

Albert William Kaline was born on December 19, 1934, the only son of Nicholas and Naomi Kaline, who lived on Cedley Street in Baltimore's Westport neighborhood. Al had two older sisters, Margaret and Caroline. His father, a broom maker, and his uncles Bib and Fred had all played semiprofessional ball. As a boy, Al wanted nothing more than to become a big leaguer like his idol Ted Williams of the Red Sox.

Although Al was smaller than other boys his age, he loved baseball and spent hours developing his skills. He also played softball and basketball, but baseball remained his favorite sport.

In 1949, as a fifteen-year-old freshman at Southern High School, Al tried out for the football team. Despite his concerns about the boy's slim build, the coach gave the 5-foot, 7-inch, 115-pound Kaline a spot on the squad. When Al broke his cheekbone in midseason, his football days ended.

At Southern High's baseball tryouts that spring, coach Bill Anderson also thought the freshman was too small; Al still weighed less than 120 pounds. But he returned day after day, pleading for an opportunity to play any position. Finally, Anderson relented, allowing the eager kid to try out.

The coach immediately noticed Al's excellent batting form and his strong throwing arm; despite Kaline's small size, he threw with speed and accuracy. Al made the team, but at first he merely warmed the bench as he watched the veteran players.

When Southern High's starting center fielder broke his leg, Al got his chance. He ran down a screaming line drive to deep left center. Impressed with Kaline's skill and intensity, his teammate Charley Johnson introduced Al to Walter Youse, the manager of the Westport American Legion team.

Kaline made the 1950 Legion team, hitting .333 and landing a spot on the All-Star American Legion junior team. While other kids took odd jobs, Nicholas Kaline discouraged his son from working. Instead, he urged Al to play as much baseball as possible that summer, hoping the boy would gain valuable playing experience. His uncles Bib and Fred chauffeured their nephew all over the city as he changed uniforms in the car between games played on pickup squads or with a recreational league and an industrial nine. Al even attended a Brooklyn Dodgers tryout camp, but was rejected and advised to gain weight.

As his sophomore year began, Kaline followed a strict training regimen of good food and exercise. By the spring of 1951, he weighed 135 pounds and had sprouted up to 5 feet, 11 inches. He'd attracted the attention of scouts, including Ed Katalinas of the Tigers, who watched him excel at second base and center field.

The *Baltimore News-Post* named the slugging sophomore to the annual Hearst Sandlot Game in New York City. Playing in the Polo Grounds, the skinny Baltimore kid hit two singles before lining a home run into the upper-deck grandstand in left field. Named the game's Most Valuable Player, Al was awarded the Lou Gehrig trophy for all-around excellence. The following day, Kaline saw his first big league game at Yankee Stadium, where he watched Mickey Mantle and company take on the St. Louis Browns.

Returning to Baltimore, he played for the Legion team once more, batting .609 with a slugging average of .891. Years later, manager Walter Youse observed, "In all the years I coached Legion ball, Al Kaline was the finest all-around player I handled."

By his junior year in 1952, Al weighed 160 pounds. He'd also become an excellent basketball player, scoring an average 22.5 points per game, but baseball remained his game. That spring he hit .469 and made the Maryland All-Scholastic team. Al batted .427 and stole 20 bases in his senior year at Southern High. He became the first Baltimore student to make the All-Scholastic team in four consecutive years.

Al graduated from high school on June 17, 1953. The next morning Ed Katalinas visited the Kalines' home on Cedley Street and Al signed a contract with the Tigers for $30,000. Baseball rules required that any team giving a player more than a $6,000 signing bonus had to keep him on the major league team for two years. This hurt many players who would have benefited from playing in the minors, but Kaline was not one of them.

Although it was unusual for a rookie to go directly to the big leagues, the Tigers had high hopes for Al. On Monday, June 24, Katalinas drove Kaline from Baltimore to Philadelphia's Shibe Park where Detroit was playing the Philadelphia A's. Later Kaline admitted to being scared stiff. "But I had desire. Desire is something you must have to make it in the majors. I was never satisfied with just average."

Katalinas introduced the shy Kaline to Detroit skipper Fred Hutchinson, a former pitcher known for his quick-tempered, competitive managerial style. The clubhouse manager showed the rookie his locker and handed him a new uniform with number 6 on it. Kaline met other young Tigers: Bob Miller, Frank House, Harvey Kuenn, and

After starring at Southern High School in Baltimore, Al Kaline went directly to the major leagues, never playing in the minors.

third baseman Reno Bertoia, who would become his roommate and friend. He was introduced to the club's veterans Steve Souchock, Don Lund, Johnny Pesky, Walt Dropo, and Gerry Priddy.

Kaline watched the first game from the bench, but the following evening Hutchinson sent him out to right field in the eighth inning. Although the rookie had never played right field, he grabbed his glove without a word and bounded out of the dugout, joining Jim Delsing in left and Don Lund in center. He followed Lund's signals, shifting to the left or right for various hitters, but nothing came his way. As he ran off the field he realized he would be the leadoff batter. Like an old pro, Number 6 grabbed his 34-ounce bat and stepped up to the plate to face the A's hurler. Announcing his arrival in the big leagues, Kaline met the first pitch and smacked a hard liner directly to the center fielder, who caught it easily.

When the club returned to Detroit, outfielders Steve Souchock and Pat Mullin instructed Kaline on defensive play. Second baseman Johnny Pesky tutored him on offense, honing his bunting skills and teaching the kid to pull the ball to left or slap it to right field. Kaline later credited Pesky with teaching him the most about the game.

When they played Boston in September, Hutch asked Ted Williams to talk with Kaline. The great Red Sox hitter readily obliged. He showed Kaline some hitting exercises, gave him tips on judging sliders and curves, and suggested strategies for hitting with two strikes. "Go up on the bat and protect the plate," he said. "Choke it just a little, but make sure you've got that whole strike zone in range."

Next he showed the rookie how to adjust to lower and higher pitches in the strike zone. But Williams repeatedly emphasized one point: "Get a good pitch. You hear me? Get a good pitch."

Although Kaline played in only thirty games his first year, he made a favorable impression with the Tigers. He also hit his first home run off right-hander Dave Hooskins in Cleveland. At the end of the season

In addition to his hitting, Kaline was an outstanding outfielder. He twice played an entire season without making an error.

he returned to the quieter life of Baltimore, where he worked in a sporting goods store. In December Kaline became engaged to his high school sweetheart, Louise Hamilton.

Following Ted Williams's advice, throughout the winter Kaline swung a 70-ounce stunt bat each morning for thirty minutes and squeezed a baseball to strengthen his arms.

Reporting to spring training in 1954, Kaline had grown to 6 feet, 1 inch and weighed 175 pounds. Steve Souchock had broken his wrist playing winter ball and Hutch made Kaline his starting right fielder. In April the Tigers played the White Sox at Briggs Stadium (as Tiger Stadium was then called). During the game Kaline threw three men out from right field, prompting a sportswriter to observe, "And when required to sprint for the catch, the Detroit hero was none-too-slow either." Suddenly, everyone in Detroit knew about the young Tiger.

Late in the season Kaline spent five days in the hospital after spraining his right knee when he crashed into an outfield corner. He finished the year batting .276. Two weeks after the season ended, he and Louise were married at St. John's Lutheran Church in Baltimore.

By opening day 1955 Kaline had become a Tiger fixture. Fans, teammates, and writers often referred to him merely as Six, his number. On April 17, 1955, Detroit hosted the Kansas City Athletics. In the third inning the A's John Gray delivered a curve that Kaline sent into the lower deck of the left field stands.

In the sixth, Kaline met a fastball and smacked it 400 feet into the upper deck of the left field stands. Nine Tigers batted in that inning; when Kaline came up again he hit another one into the left field lower deck. Kaline became the first Detroit player to hit two home runs in the same inning.

The last American League player to achieve that feat was Joe Di-Maggio in 1936; he was impressed by Kaline. "This kid can't miss being one of the greatest all-round players of all time. He's got that extra special look that you hear about, but seldom see."

The twenty-year-old Kaline ended the '55 season with a .340 batting average, enough to make him the youngest player ever to win the American League batting crown. Before Kaline, Detroit's legendary Ty Cobb had held the record, but Cobb's December 18 birthday made him one day older than the Tigers newest slugger. "We may be seeing in this kid the greatest hitter of all time," said Detroit coach Billy Hitchcock. "Everything he does is exactly right."

By the end of the season, Al and Louise, who made Detroit their home, welcomed the birth of their first child, Mark. Two years later, their second child, Michael, was born.

The Tigers remained a mediocre club through the late '50s and early '60s. In 1963, Charlie Dressen, a former third baseman and a veteran coach and manager, took the helm until he suffered a heart attack in 1965. Dressen returned to managing, but the Tigers were stunned when Dressen died on August 10, 1966, following a second heart attack. The team was dealt yet another blow when Dressen's replacement, Bob Swift, died on October 17.

The Tigers began to improve under the guidance of their new skipper, Mayo Smith. Now known as Mr. Tiger, Kaline played an important role in the club's growth. Detroit pitcher Johnny Podres, who joined the club in 1966, praised his teammate's consistency, "You almost have to watch him play every day to appreciate what he does. You hear about him sure, but you really can't understand until you see him. He just never makes a mistake."

Many observers expected the Tigers to win the American League pennant in 1967, but injuries to two key players greatly hampered the team during the latter part of the season. In September, pitching ace Denny McLain injured his foot and was out of the rotation. And, in a rare outburst of anger, Kaline jammed his bat into the bat rack after

During his twenty-two years as a Detroit Tiger, Kaline collected 3007 hits. He led the league in batting when he was only twenty.

striking out against Cleveland's Sam McDowell and broke his hand. He later described the incident as " the stupidest thing I ever did."

But 1968 became "the year of the Tiger." The entire season seemed magical. Detroit's outfielder, Jim Northrup, hit three grand slams during five days in June—two in one game. Denny McClain became the first 30-game winner since the Cardinals Dizzy Dean in 1934. The Tigers led the league on all but fifteen days, clinching the pennant on September 17.

Detroit faced a tough battle against the Cardinals in the 1968 World Series, a rematch of the 1934 contest that Detroit had lost to St. Louis. Tigers manager Mayo Smith made a bold move on the eve of the Series by switching center fielder Mickey Stanley to shortstop to get Al Kaline's bat into the lineup.

Smith's gamble paid off. Stanley's play was dazzling and Kaline delivered key hits in the Tigers' 7-game victory, batting .379 with 2 homers and 8 RBI.

The city of Detroit celebrated its bicentennial in 1969. Fans selected an all-time Tigers team, including Kaline, Hank Greenberg, Charlie Gehringer, Billy Rogell, George Kell, Ty Cobb, Harry Heilmann, Mickey Cochrane, Hal Newhouser, and Denny McClain.

In 1972 Detroit mounted another fight for the American League pennant. Three years earlier the major leagues had split into two divisions; the division winners played for the pennant. After winning the American League East by a half-game over the Red Sox, Detroit faced the Oakland A's, winners in the West. The Tigers bowed to Oakland in five games.

The Tigers finished third in 1973 and dropped to fifth place in 1974. Kaline, thirty-nine, retired. Mr. Tiger had given the club his best for twenty-two years. In Kaline's long tenure with Detroit, the Tigers finished higher than third only six times, and won just one pennant. He had played for fourteen managers. Many years he was plagued by

Kaline goes into the stands after a line drive by the Yankees Elston Howard.

injuries—he'd broken his cheek, his collarbone, his hand, and his arm—but Kaline overcame these obstacles to win ten Gold Gloves and appear in fourteen All-Star games. "Kaline made playing right field into an art form," wrote Richard Tourangeau. "All comparisons to his glove work eventually fell short because he was graceful and quick. Never a wasted motion, never a wrong decision. All his baseball skills were impeccably honed: hitting for power and average, speed, throwing, and fielding judgment."

Kaline's contributions to the Tigers offense were outstanding; he retired with 3,007 hits, a .297 career batting average, and 399 homers. Among Hall of Fame right fielders, Kaline ranks third in slugging average behind Babe Ruth and the Cubs Billy Williams.

In 1976, Kaline began broadcasting Detroit games on television. He has called Tiger games for over twenty years. Kaline was inducted into Baseball's Hall of Fame in 1980. Discussing his career in baseball he told an interviewer, "I showed up, I played, and I loved it."

Further Readings

Gilbert, Thomas. *Baseball and the the Color Line.* New York: Franklin Watts, 1995.

Gilbert, Thomas. *Dead Ball: Major League Baseball Before Babe Ruth.* New York: Franklin Watts, 1996.

Gilbert, Thomas. *The Good Old Days: Baseball in the 1930s.* New York: Franklin Watts, 1996.

Hirshberg, Al. *The Al Kaline Story.* New York: Julian Messner, Inc.,1964.

Macht, Norman L. *Babe Ruth.* Philadelphia: Chelsea House Publishers, 1991.

Macht, Norman L. *Jimmie Foxx.* Philadelphia: Chelsea House Publishers, 1991.

McKissack, Patricia. *Black Diamond: The Story of the Negro Leagues.* New York: Scholastic, 1994.

Nicholson, Lois P. *Babe Ruth: Sultan of Swat.* Woodbury, Conn.: Goodwood, 1994.

Riley, James A. *The Negro Leagues.* Philadelphia: Chelsea House Publishers, 1997.

Ward, Geoffrey C., and Ken Burns. *Baseball: 25 Great Moments.* New York: Alfred A. Knopf, 1994.

Ward, Geoffrey C., and Ken Burns. *Shadow Ball: The History of the Negro Leagues.* New York: Alfred A. Knopf, 1994.

Ward, Geoffrey C., and Ken Burns. *Who Invented the Game?* New York: Alfred A. Knopf, 1994.

Sources

Astor, Gerald. *The Baseball Hall of Fame 50th Anniversary Book*. New York: Prentice Hall Press, 1988.

Cantor, George. *The Tigers of '68: Baseball's Last Real Champions*. Dallas, Texas: Taylor Publishing, 1997.

Clark, Dick, and Larry Lester, editors. *The Negro Leagues Book*. Cleveland: The Society for American Baseball Research, 1994.

Cochrane, Gordon S. (Mickey). *Baseball: The Fan's Game*. 1939. Reprinted, Cleveland: The Society for American Baseball Research, 1992.

Creamer, Rober W. *Babe: The Legend Comes To Life*. New York: Simon and Schuster, 1974.

Falls, Joe. *The Detroit Tigers: An Illustrated History*. New York: Walker and Company, 1989.

Gardner, Robert, and Dennis Shortelle. *The Forgotten Players: The Story of Black Baseball in America*. New York: Walker and Company, 1993.

Gerlach, Larry. *The Men In Blue: Conversations with Umpires*. New York: Viking, 1980.

Holway, John B. *Blackball Stars: Negro League Pioneers*. Westport, Conn.: Meckler Books, 1988.

Holway, John B. *Life in the Negro Leagues from Men Who Lived It*. Westport, Conn.: Meckler Books, 1989.

Keetz, Frank. "Town Team Ball." *The National Pastime: A Review of Baseball History*, no. 16 (1996).

Mowbray, William W. *The Eastern Shore Baseball League.* Centreville, Maryland: Tidewater Publishers, 1989.

Peterson, Robert. *Only the Ball Was White: A History of Legendary Black Players and All-Black Professional Teams Before Black Men Played in the Major Leagues.* New York: McGraw-Hill Book Company, 1970.

Statistics

John Franklin "Home Run" Baker

Philadelphia Athletics, New York Yankees

Major League Batting Statistics

YEAR	TM/L	G	AB	R	H	2B	3B	HR	RBI	BB	SO	BA	SB
1908	Phi–A	9	31	5	9	3	0	0	2	0		.290	0
1909		148	541	73	165	27	19	4	85	26		.305	20
1910		146	561	83	159	25	15	2	74	34		.283	21
1911		148	592	96	198	42	14	11	115	40		.334	38
1912		149	577	116	200	40	21	10	130	50		.347	40
1913		149	564	116	190	34	9	12	117	63	31	.337	34
1914		150	570	84	182	23	10	9	89	53	37	.319	19
1916	NY–A	100	360	46	97	23	2	10	52	36	30	.269	15
1917		146	553	57	156	24	2	6	71	48	27	.282	18
1918		126	504	65	154	24	5	6	62	38	13	.306	8
1919		141	567	70	166	22	1	10	83	44	18	.293	13
1921		94	330	46	97	16	2	9	71	26	12	.294	8
1922		69	234	30	65	12	3	7	36	15	14	.278	1
Total	13	1,575	5,984	887	1,838	315	103	96	987	473	182	.307	235
World Series (6 years)		25	91	15	33	7	0	3	18	5	11	.363	1

James Emory "Double X" Foxx

Philadelphia Athletics, Boston Red Sox, Chicago Cubs, Philadelphia Blue Jays (now Phillies)

Major League Batting Statistics

YEAR	TM/L	G	AB	R	H	2B	3B	HR	RBI	BB	SO	BA	SB
1925	Phi–A	10	9	2	6	1	0	0	0	0	1	.667	0
1926		26	32	8	10	2	1	0	5	1	6	.313	1
1927		61	130	23	42	6	5	3	20	14	11	.323	2
1928		118	400	85	131	29	10	13	79	60	43	.327	3
1929		149	517	123	183	23	9	33	118	103	70	.354	9
1930		153	562	127	188	33	13	37	156	93	66	.335	7
1931		139	515	93	150	32	10	30	120	73	84	.291	4
1932		154	585	151	213	33	9	58	169	116	96	.364	3
1933		149	573	125	204	37	9	48	163	96	93	.356	2
1934		150	539	120	180	28	6	44	130	111	75	.334	11
1935		147	535	118	185	33	7	36	115	114	99	.346	6
1936	Bos–A	155	585	130	198	32	8	41	143	105	119	.338	13
1937		150	569	111	162	24	6	36	127	99	96	.285	10
1938		149	565	139	197	33	9	50	175	119	76	.349	5
1939		124	467	130	168	31	10	35	105	89	72	.360	4
1940		144	515	106	153	30	4	36	119	101	87	.297	4
1941		135	487	87	146	27	8	19	105	93	103	.300	2
1942	Bos–A	30	100	18	27	4	0	5	14	18	15	.270	0
	Chi–N	70	205	25	42	8	0	3	19	22	55	.205	1
1944		15	20	0	1	1	0	0	2	2	5	.050	0
1945	Phi–N	89	224	30	60	11	1	7	38	23	39	.268	0
Total	20	2,317	8,134	1,751	2,646	458	125	534	1,922	1,452	1,311	.325	87
World Series (3 years)		18	64	11	22	3	1	4	11	9	10	.344	0

(Foxx did not play in 1943.)

Robert Moses "Lefty" Grove
Philadelphia Athletics, Boston Red Sox
Major League Pitching Statistics

YEAR	TM/L	W	L	PCT	G	GS	CG	SH	IP	H	BB	SO	ERA
1925	Phi–A	10	12	.455	45	18	5	0	197	207	131	116	4.75
1926		13	13	.500	45	33	20	1	258	227	101	194	2.51
1927		20	13	.606	51	28	14	1	262	251	79	174	3.19
1928		24	8	.750	39	31	24	4	261	228	64	183	2.58
1929		20	6	.769	42	37	19	2	275	278	81	170	2.81
1930		28	5	.848	50	32	22	2	291	273	60	209	2.54
1931		31	4	.886	41	30	27	4	288	249	62	175	2.06
1932		25	10	.714	44	30	27	4	291	269	79	188	2.84
1933		24	8	.750	45	28	21	2	275	280	83	114	3.20
1934	Bos–A	8	8	.500	22	12	5	0	109	149	32	43	6.50
1935		20	12	.625	35	30	23	2	273	269	65	121	2.70
1936		17	12	.586	35	30	22	6	253	237	65	130	2.81
1937		17	9	.654	32	32	21	3	262	269	83	153	3.02
1938		14	4	.778	24	21	12	1	163	169	52	99	3.08
1939		15	4	.789	23	23	17	2	191	180	58	81	2.54
1940		7	6	.538	22	21	9	1	153	159	50	62	3.99
1941		7	7	.500	21	21	10	0	134	155	42	54	4.37
Total	17	300	141	.680	616	457	298	35	3,940	3,849	1,187	2,266	3.06
World Series (3 years)		4	2	.667	8	5	4	0	51	46	6	36	1.75

William Julius "Judy" Johnson
Madison Stars, Philadelphia Hilldales, Pittsburgh Homestead Grays,
Philadelphia Hilldales, Pittsburgh Crawfords
Negro League Batting Statistics

YEAR	TM/L	G	AB	H	2B	3B	HR	BA	SB
1919	Mad– Stars	1	4	0	0	0	0	.000	0
1920	No data available								
1921	Phi–Hilldales	22	88	20	3	2	2	.227	1
1922		7	25	2	0	0	0	.080	0
1923		27	86	31	12	1	1	.360	2
1924		71	245	84	19	6	2	.343	4
1925		66	249	97	12	8	4	.390	7
1926		87	339	111	21	6	2	.327	14
1927		51	183	49	5	2	1	.268	2
1928		52	205	46	3	3	1	.224	0
1929		74	256	104	13	1	3	.406	12
1930	Homestead Grays	16	69	19	0	1	0	.275	
1931	Phi–Hilldales	56	205	56	3	3	0	.273	2
1932	2 teams Phi–Hilldales, Pit–Crawfords								
	Total	32	115	31	2	4	1	.270	2
1933	Pit–Crawfords	36	121	27	8	0	0	.223	0
1934		50	192	49	9	3	1	.255	2
1935		55	222	68	12	3	1	.306	2
1936		25	88	22	3	1	0	.250	1
Total	18	728	2,692	816	125	44	19	.303	51

Albert William "Al" Kaline
Detroit Tigers
Major League Batting Statistics

YEAR	TM/L	G	AB	R	H	2B	3B	HR	RBI	BB	SO	BA	SB
1953	Det–A	30	28	9	7	0	0	1	2	1	5	.250	1
1954		138	504	42	139	18	3	4	43	22	45	.276	9
1955		152	588	121	200	24	8	27	102	82	57	.340	6
1956		153	617	96	194	32	10	27	128	70	55	.314	7
1957		149	577	83	170	29	4	23	90	43	38	.295	11
1958		146	543	84	170	34	7	16	85	54	47	.313	7
1959		136	511	86	167	19	2	27	94	72	42	.327	10
1960		147	551	77	153	29	4	15	68	65	47	.278	19
1961		153	586	116	190	41	7	19	82	66	42	.324	14
1962		100	398	78	121	16	6	29	94	47	39	.304	4
1963		145	551	89	172	24	3	27	101	54	48	.312	6
1964		146	525	77	154	31	5	17	68	75	51	.293	4
1965		125	399	72	112	18	2	18	72	72	49	.281	6
1966		142	479	85	138	29	1	29	88	81	66	.288	5
1967		131	458	94	141	28	2	25	78	83	47	.308	8
1968		102	327	49	94	14	1	10	53	55	39	.287	6
1969		131	456	74	124	17	0	21	69	54	61	.272	1
1970		131	467	64	130	24	4	16	71	77	49	.278	2
1971		133	405	69	119	19	2	15	54	82	57	.294	4
1972		106	278	46	87	11	2	10	32	28	33	.313	1
1973		91	310	40	79	13	0	10	45	29	28	.255	4
1974		147	558	71	146	28	2	13	64	65	75	.262	2
Total	22	2,834	10,116	1,622	3,007	498	75	399	1,583	1,277	1,020	.297	137
World Series (1 year)		7	29	6	11	2	0	2	8	0	7	.379	0

George Herman "Babe" Ruth
Boston Red Sox, New York Yankees, Boston Braves
Major League Batting Statistics

YEAR	TM/L	G	AB	R	H	2B	3B	HR	RBI	BB	SO	BA	SB
1914	Bos–A	5	10	1	2	1	0	0	2	0	4	.200	0
1915		42	92	16	29	10	1	4	21	9	23	.315	0
1916		67	136	18	37	5	3	3	15	10	23	.272	0
1917		52	123	14	40	6	3	2	12	12	18	.325	0
1918		95	317	50	95	26	11	11	66	57	58	.300	6
1919		130	432	103	139	34	12	29	114	101	58	.322	7
1920	NY–A	142	458	158	172	36	9	54	137	148	80	.376	14
1921		152	540	177	204	44	16	59	171	144	81	.378	17
1922		110	406	94	128	24	8	35	99	84	80	.315	2
1923		152	522	151	205	45	13	41	131	170	83	.393	17
1924		153	529	143	200	39	7	46	121	142	81	.378	9
1925		98	359	61	104	12	2	25	66	59	68	.290	2
1926		152	495	139	184	30	5	47	146	144	76	.372	11
1927		151	540	158	192	29	8	60	164	138	89	.356	7
1928		154	536	163	173	29	8	54	142	135	87	.323	4
1929		135	499	121	172	26	6	46	154	72	60	.345	5
1930		145	518	150	186	28	9	49	153	136	61	.359	10
1931		145	534	149	199	31	3	46	163	128	51	.373	5
1932		133	457	120	156	13	5	41	137	130	62	.341	2
1933		137	459	97	138	21	3	34	103	114	90	.301	4
1934		125	365	78	105	17	4	22	84	103	63	.288	1
1935	Bos–N	28	72	13	13	0	0	6	12	20	24	.181	0
Total	22	2,503	8,399	2,174	2,873	506	136	714	2,213	2,056	1,330	.342	123
World Series (10 years)		41	129	37	42	5	2	15	33	33	30	.326	4

George Herman "Babe" Ruth
Boston Red Sox, New York Yankees
Major League Pitching Statistics

YEAR	TM/L	W	L	PCT	G	GS	CG	SH	IP	H	BB	SO	ERA
1914	Bos–A	2	1	.667	4	3	1	0	23	21	7	3	3.91
1915		18	8	.692	32	28	16	1	217	166	85	112	2.44
1916		23	12	.657	44	41	23	9	323	230	118	170	1.75
1917		24	13	.649	41	38	35	6	326	244	108	128	2.01
1918		13	7	.650	20	19	18	1	166	125	49	40	2.22
1919		9	5	.643	17	15	12	0	133	148	58	30	2.97
1920	NY–A	1	0	1.000	1	1	0	0	4	3	2	0	4.50
1921		2	0	1.000	2	1	0	0	9	14	9	2	9.00
1930		1	0	1.000	1	1	1	0	9	11	2	3	3.00
1933		1	0	1.000	1	1	1	0	9	12	3	0	5.00
Total	10	94	46	.671	163	148	107	17	1,221	974	441	488	2.28
World Series (2 years)		3	0	1.000	3	3	2	1	31	19	10	8	0.87

Victor Gazaway "Vic" Willis
Boston Beaneaters, Pittsburgh Pirates, St. Louis Cardinals
Major League Pitching Statistics

YEAR	TM/L	W	L	PCT	G	GS	CG	SH	IP	H	BB	SO	ERA
1898	Bos–N	25	13	.658	41	38	29	1	311	264	148	160	2.84
1899		27	8	.771	41	38	35	5	342	277	117	120	2.50
1900		10	17	.370	32	29	22	2	236	258	106	53	4.19
1901		20	17	.541	38	35	33	6	305	262	78	133	2.36
1902		27	20	.574	51	46	45	4	410	372	101	225	2.20
1903		12	18	.400	33	32	29	2	278	256	88	125	2.98
1904		18	25	.419	43	43	39	2	350	357	109	196	2.85
1905		12	29	.293	41	41	36	4	342	340	107	149	3.21
1906	Pit–N	23	13	.639	41	36	32	6	322	295	76	124	1.73
1907		21	11	.656	39	37	27	6	292	234	69	107	2.34
1908		23	11	.676	41	38	25	7	304	239	69	97	2.07
1909		22	11	.667	39	35	24	4	289	243	83	95	2.24
1910	StL–N	9	12	.429	33	23	12	1	212	224	61	67	3.35
Total	13	249	205	.548	513	471	388	50	3,996	3,621	1,212	1,651	2.63
World Series (1 year)		0	1	.000	2	1	0	0	11	10	8	3	4.76

Index

INDEX